Wychwood Forest and its Border Places

See! dawn breaks, painting leaf and tree.
Old Wychwood dons its robe of green;
Now, at our feet, what joy to see
Its rolling sweep of glorious sheen.

Fair scenes; here beast and bird
Find safe retreat 'gainst man's alarm;
Rare blossoms too, by lake and sward,
Come to perfection, safe from harm.

The cover photograph is reproduced from 'Newell Plain in Wychwood Forest, Oxfordshire' (1854) by William Turner of Oxford (1789-1862) by permission of the Williamson Art Gallery and Museum, Birkenhead.

ST. SYTHA, SITHA, CITHA, &c.
Wall painting at Shorthampton Church.

Wychwood Forest
and its Border Places

John Kibble

With an Introduction by Roy Townsend

The Wychwood Press

PUBLISHER'S NOTE

John Kibble expressed the view that the information in his books was every-body's property, and he did not want it to be the subject of copyright. He would not have been able to write his books, he said, without the help of a great number of local people who told him their stories or showed him family documents.

However, we would like to acknowledge our debt to this endearing historian and raconteur by contributing a royalty from the sale of each book to the Victoria History of Oxfordshire Appeal, a cause which would have been close to Kibble's heart, particularly since much of the work that remains to be done is in West Oxfordshire.

A note about the text

The text in this edition is virtually unchanged from the original. A few of what are obviously mis-spellings or printer's errors have been corrected, but they have only served to point to the fact that Kibble did not proof read his books as metic-ulously as he should. The careful reader will note that in the present volume he spells his own grandfather's name in two ways...

Nor was he over-zealous in arranging the entries in alphabetical order. The book is more a collection of notes, fairly casually arranged, and evidently written partly in Charlbury and partly in Finstock.

Except for the photograph on page x, the illustrations are from the original edition. The artist(s) is/are not acknowledged but as some are initialled JK and Kibble elsewhere expresses his gratitude to his art teacher at school, they are almost certainly his own.

J.C.

First published 1928 by John Kibble, 'The Firs', Charlbury

Second edition with minor typographical corrections only, 1999

Published by The Wychwood Press, an imprint of Jon Carpenter Publishing,
2 The Spendlove Centre, Charlbury OX7 3DA
Telephone and fax 01608 811969

Printed in Bristol by J W Arrowsmith Ltd

Contents

Foreword

by Roy Townsend

John Kibble was a stone mason, a local historian, and a Methodist lay preacher. He had a great interest in the past, and a desire to recount and share his considerable knowledge.

My first memories of him are from when I was a young lad and had to attend the local Methodist chapel in Finstock. To the children he seemed a tall man, and his pocket watch held a great fascination as we waited for him to check the time of his watch with the chapel clock.

He was interested in the young people and always had something to show us. Sometimes it would be a flint arrowhead he had found, on another occasion it was a 'patten' that people used to wear on their shoes to keep them out of the mud. There was always the invitation to keep our eyes open and see what *we* could find — and when one of us found something, to "let me have a little peep".

As we walked with him after the service he would point out many things of interest. Just outside the chapel there was the site of the old well that gave its name to Well Hill, and he'd show us the cottage where he was born and spent his childhood. He would tell us how he had to journey to Charlbury to collect medicines for the villagers, and how much he loved doing this — especially if it meant a day off school! He was so very proud of being born and brought up in Finstock and could often be heard to say, "Oh my, oh my, how I love Finstock!"

In his younger days Wychwood Forest was always open for people to walk in and through, but by the time he was old enough to walk in it himself, it had become a closed, forbidden place, out of bounds to all who had been used to its pleasures as well as for those who had yet to experience such delights. He would be thrilled today to be able to walk through once again, to see the wild flowers and the different trees, and hear the birds singing and see the wildlife. But his joy would be tempered, I am sure, with sadness that so many of the wild flowers of his youth have disappeared.

As to modern car use, he would say it undermines family life, and he would have a very sharp remark to make about the light pollution that makes it so difficult to see the stars.

His books, which he originally published himself, have encouraged old and young alike to take a greater interest in local history, the customs and daily pracctices of a bygone way of life, and to delve and investigate and thereby learn more of their ancestors and how they lived.

Chairman, Finstock Local History Group
Finstock, July 1998

Wychwood Forest

and its Border Places

Two plaques are attached to this fountain, situated in the Playing Close in Charlbury. One reads: "This fountain is erected to commemorate the visit of HM Queen Victoria to Charlbury in Nov 1886, the provision of a water supply for the town in 1896, the 60th anniversary of the Queen's accession June 20 1897". The second records that "This fountain was designed and built by John Kibble of Charlbury 1865-1951". Kibble's gravestone in the cemetery records that "John Kibble [was] called home Dec 18th 1951 aged 86 years" and also commemorates "his wife Florence, called home April 13th 1952 aged 85 years" and "their daughter Kathleen Ann, 19th July 1896 - 3rd Feb 1971".

Introduction

My attempt at book making, *Notes on Charlbury and its Hamlets*, seems to have met a need, and has brought me much kindness from peer to peasant; and something being said about 'more', which I can give, I am venturing again with Notes, having Wychwood Forest as a centre or pivot on which to hang them.

It was my good fortune to first see the light on the forest borders at Finstock, so the glamour and charm of Wychwood was from earliest days upon me. This was owing to hearing it constantly referred to on all hands, and especially by my father, who knew almost every yard of it. The pheasants had not been installed when he was a boy, and he lovingly regarded it as the playground and fairyland of his youth. He said: 'Lord Churchill was most pleased to see all about him enjoying the delights of the place, and so you "kept your foot in your shoe". You were heartily welcome.'

To me the forest was a forbidden place; we could see it, and look across its glorious sweep, to High Lodge away against the sky, from the Heath above Finstock. I saw a good bit of Cornbury Park, as I used to be sent pretty frequently down to the doctor at Charlbury for medicine, carrying it carefully and safely always, never had a spill (how glad I am), for neighbours and friends. School was not possible those mornings, but whilst my companions had the benefit of school lessons, at which they shone better than I did, mine was the joy of the open air, sun and wind, or storm; and bird, leaf and tree; which, to a sickly boy, no doubt was better than a crowded school room.

Over the Paddock Stile, at Finstock, down the Cow Pasture, where, long before, an earthquake tremor had, I heard, been felt, up through Molly Fawdry's Copse, along West Fields, down the Little Park, over the Pond Head, along the Big Park past the mound with a ponderous oak tree on top of it, under the walnut tree where the farmer had fought and killed the shepherd, away on over the Ladder Stile, close to the Lodge, where had lived the man who had the bacon for minding his own business and leaving other people's alone, on over the Bridges, and so to Charlbury. Then the journey home; sometimes by the coach road, out at the Green Gates, it was tip top.

> 'It brings to me my childhood days
> As if I trod its very track
> And felt its very gladness.'

I saw something of Wychwood Forest and its border places later on, for when the desire of my early days was realised, and I could go with my father to work at the various places he had told me many a story about, then I had joy indeed.

Father asked if he could go through the forest to and from work, when it lay the opposite side from Finstock, and this was a consideration to a mason walking, and sometimes carrying tools. He had worked at Barcheston Church, near Shipston on Stour, beginning work at seven a.m., hearing Charlbury Church clock strike three, perhaps, as he walked down Pound Hill, a few feet from where I write.

We used to start Monday morning very early. How bright and crisp it was, wishing mother, dear good mother, 'good-bye' for the week — and away down Patch Riding past the old Pest House and the gateway where there used to be stone pillars and balls, called 'The Knobs' by elderly Finstock people to this day, and through the forbidden gate near to which a bullet once had missed a man, I heard, down to the Dog Kennels, where was the old Quarry from which had come stone for the Guildhall, London, and Blenheim Palace. Presently we struck the Big Light, and away.

The morning, the sky, the forest (and to be in it), youth, the mason's art, the wonderful men (how friendly and jolly they were), the villages, the lodgings, and the best chum I ever had, my father — life was good, if hard.

Later on in frosty weather I would set off and visit some old church, and without a word to anyone see all I could. Walk? Yes, that beats all other modes of travel for enjoying a bit of dear old Oxfordshire — roads, lanes, footpaths, brooks, and villages.

So one way and another I have seen a good bit of the forest and its setting. Sometimes we went other routes, swiftly walking along, also staying for some time at some of the border places. I trod the 'primrose path of rural life', and found that very much pleasure may be most inexpensive; and that hard toil and plain, simple fare need not mean wretchedness by a long way, even if to some of us the *master* word of life was, *work*.

Though the acres were not mine, every prospect, hill and dale, tree and stream, I had an interest in them, and have lovingly tried to set down gleanings and happenings that have come to me, a Wychwood village lad.

I have gleaned in many fields. The Cartularies of Eynsham Abbey have much about Wychwood and its border places, and Mr. Watney's superb book, Cornbury and Wychwood, must have grateful mention.

My best thanks to the authorities of Brasenose College, Oxford, per Mr. Coxhill, for some of the information given re Charlbury Grammar School, and to all who have helped to make this book possible.

As King Alfred said when he issued a book, so would I say: 'I beg every reader to pray for me and not to blame me ... every man must according to the measure of his understanding and according to his leisure, speak what he speaketh, and do what he doeth.'

Wychwood Forest

The Forest of Witchwood beareth a great breadth and in time past spread far wider. For King Richard III. dissaforested the great Territory of Witchwood between Woodstock and Brightstow which Edward the Fourth made to be a Forest.

Camden 1634.

William who loved the chase had 68 forests, and Wychwood was one of the four largest in the land. A park had palings or a wall, but a forest, metes and bounds, and spread far and wide, as did Wychwood.

HWICCEWUDU, 841. WYEWUD. HUCHEWODE. WICCHEWODE.

It has been thought that the name came from the name of a tribe of early men in the West of England, but beyond the name HICWIC, there does not seem anything to support this.

From earliest time salt springs were Wic, Wicks, or Wyches, and the belief was that such places approach nearest heaven, and that prayers were nowhere heard sooner of the gods.

Is there not a 'Wych' in the forest; the medicinal spring called today The Iron Well? Our forefathers looked upon such springs as a gift of the gods; it was Wic or Wyche, something beyond, uncanny.

The pilgrimage made yearly to ours was kept up from Finstock on Palm Sunday with bottles of Spanish Water till the pheasants came, and all entry to the forest was put down with a strong hand. I hear Leafield still goes bottle in hand to their Wych, the spring called Uzzel, continuing a custom lost in the ages of the past, when men looked on springs as God's gifts, especially those of healing value, and there the devout went to pray.

> Hast then a wound to heal
> The wych doth grieve thee ?
> Come then unto this welle,
> It will relieve thee:
> Nolie me tangeries,
> And other maladies
> Have here thyr remedies
> Pray'sd be the Lord.

Slate pits long barrow is not so far away; early man felt God was near a spring, it was Wych, and the wood containing it Wychwood.

Forest Law

'All persons above 12 years of age who lived within its bounds were compelled to take an oath "to be of good behaviour towards his majesties wild beasts".' They were the hart, the hind, the hare, the boar and the wolf. Only the highest in the land might kill deer. 'Game, dainty meat for the king and the best sort of men in the realm.'

All dogs kept about a forest had their fore claws cut off with chisel and mallet.

No one, not even those who had been granted the right to hunt, might do so for forty days before or after the king's hunt, so that 'the wild beasts might not by any means be disquieted of their rest and peace.'

In Saxon days the laws were severe, but when the Normans came William saw to it that all forest laws were tightened up, so not only the poor but those of high degree had to be careful how they got their venison.

If a dead deer was found an inquest was held to discover the manner of its death (if 'meete and sweete' it was given in charity) but woe betide the poor chap who killed it if unlawfully done.

If force was offered to a forest keeper death was the penalty.

The hunting instinct is very strong in some natures, and risks were taken even by Church dignitaries and men of high degree.

In 1126 Roger de Oilly is fined 200 marks and later on 20 marks.

Combe rector, Andrew de Woodstock, in his long incumbency of 44 years has recorded against him that for trespass he found himself in Oxford Castle.

In 1105 Henry I was at Cornbury and he enforced the forest laws with severity. He seems to have favoured wild beasts much, for he had a kind of zoo at Woodstock for animals too fierce and wild even for those free days.

Alan Rasur had forest rights for which he paid £10 rent in 1130-1. Richard Camville, of Stanton Harcourt fame, also had to do with HUCKEUVODE.

In 1222 fforesters, verderers, and agistors were ordered to see to the due 'agistment' of pigs, and to present the owners of swine in the forest without warrant at the forest court.

These forest courts in early days had great power. No warrant from a Justice was anything in the forest. Only forest constables and foresters were to serve, to arrest or to imprison persons there. A court sat once in three weeks, and a 'law day' once a year it is said. Men lost their eyes, limbs and heads, and the forester's axe swiftly did the work. If the offender was of low degree the limbs, etc. were hung in some conspicuous place on a gibbet as a warning; or greatly daring the dead man's friends begged the body, as one in sacred story did, and gave it decent burial.

In 1228 the king had charged to him the cartage of 6 stags and 22 deer, also a charge for salting some of our venison for his larder.

In 1230 even the great Thomas de Langlee over stepped the mark in some way and is fined £100, about £2,500 of our modern money. I wonder what he did wrong?

In 1232 Thomas is to let the men of STUNDESFULD, CUMBA, and HANEBERG turn their goats in WICHEWUDE and return them those he had impounded.

The same year William le Aleman had Maple trees for him to make mazers for the king. These wooden drinking flagons were of square shape hollowed from a small block or chunk of maple wood; old specimens are much prized today.

1154-1189

In Henry II's day Thomas Sweyn of CHERLEBYR was caught bringing an oak tree to which he had no right from the forest. He had to give a pledge that he would appear before the court. I wonder what poor Tom from Charlbury had done to him. His was not such a crime as to touch the game, so perhaps he lost only his left hand.

At that time the forest was of great extent, from Clevely across to Stanton Harcourt, and from Kidlington to Taynton, some 10 miles by 16. High Lodge was about the centre and is on the highest point, the moat which surrounds it being 631 feet above sea level.

King John is said, by Wharton, to have dug up and destroyed the Roman road, Akeman Street, in parts where it entered the forest, so as to prevent travellers using it and so passing inside his game preserve.

I wonder whether our Thomas Bassett and his son, Alan, thought of this when they stood amongst that crowd of barons with King John cornered at Runnymede that June day in 1215, when his reluctant hand put his signature to the great Charter. I fancy the elder Bassett, upright, stern and resolute, and Alan the son looking across with a slight smile to his father, thinking of Finstock, Langley and Charlbury, the places he knew so well.

The verdict of an Inquisition held in 1270 was that it would be to the king's damage if the custody of the woods of the Abbott of Eynsham within the forest of Wychwood were assigned to the bailiffs of the Abbot.

Hugh de Plessett, 1271-2, exceeded his charter which gave him permission to hunt the hare, the wolf, and the wild cat.

William de Brewen is to have 10 wild boars, 1217.

Simon de Prewes, Great Tew parson, was fined for poaching.

I saw a fine double pointed poacher's arrow found in the forest. (See p. 88.)

In Richard II's day: 'If any lay man, not having 40s. per annum: or if any priest or clerk not having living £40 per annum shall have or keep any hound, greyhound, or other dog for to hunt, or any ferrets, hays, harepipes, cords, nets, or other engines to take or destroy deere, hare, conies or other gentleman's game, and shall be convicted at the sessions of the peace, every such offender shall be imprisoned for one whole yeare.'

The forest keeper's verse for his guidance was:—

'Stable stand,

Dog draw,

Back bear,

And bloody hand.'

Anyone found standing with a weapon, or with a dog pursuing game, or carrying game on the back, or with blood on the person in the forest; in all these cases to be taken prisoner and dealt with according to forest law.

Forest Names

From Eynsham Abbey records

In 1298 a perambulation of the Forest gives names and quaint spelling: Bladenebrugge, Haneburghe, Egneisham, Canerswelle Broke, Canershulle, Frythe, Meusele, Blowynd, Osseneye, Leyhambroke, Stuntesflde, le Forakenho, Duetes feld, Grymesdiche, Spellesbury, Dychelchegge, Boxwode, Felleychegge, Wottone, Wodestok Weye, Wytteneye, Madeleyewelle, Northleye, Snellesleye, Forsakenhoke, Sigardesthorne, Sewerede, Scharpesturt, Bischopden, Tremymere, Akemanstrete, Selneyhack, Spendene, Wenerych, Faulorbrug, Stonyweye to Fynstok, Gatesdenehened, Newefryth, Wyshokes, Mereway, la Feld (Lea Field), Edwardsfeld, Eldernstub, Senkeden, Hernesgrove, Peureshulle, Stockeley, Frethereston, Quernehale, Cuttedehach, Creswey and Prestesgrove-end, Brestoneshalle, Smalestensweye, Waldene, Cockeshotehulle, Rouwehershulle, Oldlgh, Langrygyate, Asperlehurne, Merewey, Bygarsdene, Lytleswadesyate, Punfolde de Cornebery, Nunnechereche.

Many of these names can be easily recognised as being in use to-day about the forest area. Gatesdene, at Finstock, was the gate across just below the Waterloo Arms, the Lane and Well are called to-day Gadden.

Eynsham Abbey in 1307 paid 100 marks that the woods of Eynsham, Charlbury, etc., should be free from interference by the king's forest officials, but in 1366 it is stated that owing to their doings the wood, 96 acres in extent, was of no value, except to produce wood for hedges and the repair of houses.

1328. Robert de Morley had permission to chase, take, and destroy the fox, cat, badger and marten in the forest.

Edward III married at 16, settled with his wife Philippa at Woodstock. Their son, the Black Prince, was born there, so there is no doubt all the Wychwood district saw a good bit of him, and perhaps accounts for the fact that he listened to the men of Finstock when they sent a petition to him in 1349.

The forest laws were relaxed and the size reduced in 14th century.

Charles I attempted to revive the old laws in 1638, the Patent Rolls giving particulars of places that were again to be included in the forest — Idbury, Fyfield, Sarsden, Bruern with Woodstock, John Watson of that place to be steward. Perhaps it was from a desire to preserve the timber for ship building, but it soon fell through. Charles, unfortunately for his future, did some things that rankled in the minds of his people.

Just before this, 1636, one William Willoughby (good Finstock name) was fined £2,000 for felling 50 oaks worth 20s. each. Roger Gardiner (Finstock?) fined £100 for killing two does and two bucks.

The forest officials in 1792 included a ranger and 'launder', four keepers, two verderers, and a woodward. There were considered to be 1,000 head of fallow deer, the red deer had all gone some ten years before then. In 1792 it was reported the fine timber had almost disappeared, only some less than two hundred trees to be found fit for ship building.

A few years later the forest was said to be 'filled with poachers, deer stealers, thieves and pilferers of every kind, a terror to the whole country side.' A grain of salt I think would be useful here.

Enclosure and cultivation was carried out, and by 1862 large tracts were grubbed (our word for it) and much land put to the plough. Enough was left to give an idea of old English woodland scenery, and it is yet a 'haunt of ancient peace'.

The Privilege of One Day's Hunting

On the borders of Wychwood Forest there was an old custom observed by the inhabitants of hunting for one day in the forest. Whit Sunday or Monday seems to have been the day for the annual hunt. Witney had three bucks, one for Crawley, one for Hailey, and one for Witney town.

Much boisterous rowdy sport seems to have been the rule, as all and sundry almost, shared in this day's hunting. In 1573 the Government thought owing to plague or pestilence it was not wise for the assemblies to gather.

Advt. in *Jackson's Oxford Journal*

FOREST OF WYCHWOOD

Whereas at a Court held at the Ranger's Lodge in the Forest of Wychwood before the Right Hon. Lord Charles Spencer, one of the Verderers of the Forest of Wychwood, proper persons were appointed and seven Marksmen for the several

Parishes and Hamlets entitled to claim Right of Common in the said Forest:—
Now *Notice is hereby given*, That, in order to protect the rights of those who have
claims, any Cattle hereafter found in the said Forest, belonging to strangers, and
without being properly marked by the regular Marksmen, will be impounded,
and legal proceedings instituted against the owners thereof for trespass.

CHURCHILL,
Lord Warden and Ranger.

Leafield branding iron was in the possession of Mr. Howse, the blacksmith
there, and as the letters were just right he handed it to the Cricket Club of the
village, so they mark their cricket belongings with it now.

Pigs and the Swineherd's Horn

Swine were fed in the forests on acorns, beech mast, and roots, and in the
autumn the swine herd was a busy man. His stye, encircling some big spreading
tree, with a wattle fence near to water, was made ready, and littered with fern and
leaves for a comfortable bed, with a store of acorns and mast.

Collecting his herd of pigs from border places he brings the drove and puts
them into his forest sty, and at nightfall he gives them a good supper, blowing
his horn the while, so they eat to the strains he blows, and then tired and fed they
snuggle down and sleep. The next day they are taken to the water, and fed again
to the music of the horn, and after the third day the sty was opened and though
they might wander far in the day nightfall found them at the sty, or coming, especially if the horn blowing commenced.

Hawking

Hawks were trained from early British days to strike game or quarry, flying
from the wrist to do so and returning to their owners. For long the penalty was
death for killing a hawk. This was altered to imprisonment for a year and a day
with a fine at the king's pleasure as well.

Some of my earliest recollections are of a proud, imperious looking, tame
hawk with terrible beak and talons in Mr. Alderton's garden at Finstock.

Poaching Stories

It is told how one man, who shot a deer, hoisted it on to his shoulders, with
its legs hanging down each side of his neck, and started for home. As he went
trudging along he found his load began to move, for he had only wounded not
killed his venison. With a struggle and a leap, thrusting one of its feet into the
pocket of the man's trousers, and tearing the leg from top to bottom, the deer was
gone. But he had it later.

A Sharp Frost

One night the keepers came on the scene and gradually enclosed round a poacher, till presently they had him cornered down by the Evenlode. No doubt they felt pretty sure of him, but no, when he realised there was no way of escape he could see but the river he plunged in as he was and got across and made for home. It was a very sharp night, and when he arrived home his trousers were so frozen about him his wife had to use the scissors to get them from his legs. So men will venture.

* * * *

Deer were caught and snared, not always shot. Apples were temptingly hung where a buck could reach them; then he found there was a deadly secret about them, and quickly was venison.

* * * *

A man I knew said one night he was coming home to Finstock through the forest and he ran right into a deer net knocking it down. He shouted, 'Here you chaps, you must come and put your net up again, I've bin and knocked it down.' 'I knew they were about there in the bushes handy somewhere,' he said.

Straying Deer

Occasionally deer would get out of bounds, a broken fence, a field of peas; and the sight of a stray buck would fill some with a great desire to secure it, and get some venison. A man who is now dead told me some years ago about an adventure of this kind, in which one was captured and killed, it appeared. Some years back a buck jumped over the iron gates at the bottom of Pound Hill here and went away up over the Greens; the man who saw it does not know what became of it, or who had it.

'Everything That's Bad'

Some seem to be born adepts at taking game of all kinds. One youth got caught at something, and was taken in before the gentleman, and he heard, 'They tell me you can shoot. you can snare, you can fish; in fact, everything that's bad.'

Fish

There are fish in our various streams. One day my uncle caught sight of a big jack near Fawler Bridge, and borrowing a gun at the mill shot it. I remember as a lad the sight of it, and what good eating it was. I have an old poacher's home-made foul hook about 12 inches long, to be used for a jack when he lies sunning himself (or asleep perhaps?).

One man used to go, long ago, after a flood and search the pools left in the meadows with a net and forked stick. One day he got into the hands of the Blenheim keepers, and had to suffer for it. Afterwards when he got beery he used to say 'Now I'll go and knock Blenheim down.'

A Desperate Gang of Poachers

A desperate gang, led by a stonemason, a most daring man, used to carry on not far away. For a time he lived at Finstock I believe, but went to another village later. (I am glad he moved on a little). He had painted across the top of his tall hat the words 'Death or Glory', so when he went out to fight, as he often did, and threw down his hat, there was his challenge. The gang used to swear on the Book before starting on an expedition that they would not be taken. It is said that one night a very strong body of 50 keepers with dogs surrounded them, but they stood in a circle back to back and clubbed their guns, and so no thing could be done with them. All the gang, it is said, died in shame and disgrace.

Cornbury (Cornebirie)

The name seems to have been applied to all the woodland and forest in 1154. Later the name Wychwood has been used in the same inclusive way.

A park is mentioned in 1312-13.

Henry Wade held land of Edward I by the service of bringing before the king a loin of roast pork, worth 4½d., whenever he hunted in Cornebiri.

A stone house is spoken of in 1337.

In 1383 masons were to build a wall about the Queen's Park at Cornbury.

The water of Newell Brook was put to use, as were most streams formerly. Thomas Harris, a yeoman of Charlebury, gave evidence, it is recorded, that in the first year of Queen Elizabeth's reign he knew one water mill at Cornbury. Robert Saunders said he was miller there when three mills were made.

A dilapidated building used to stand at the lower lake that, I believe, had been a malt house.

The Park

There is no question as to the loveliness of Cornbury Park. Its turf; its ancient earthworks; its glorious trees, from those the Druids looked down; downwards to the Beech Avenue, 'without a rival'; the Victorian Avenue of chestnuts, with their trunks all with a twist one way, leading from the lodges to the mansion; and single specimens of thorn, hornbeam, and other trees.

The gently rising ground, gradually falling away to where the water glints through the trees. The mansion well placed in nature's setting of grass, and tree, and sky, make the motto on Clarendon's front, as I have heard it translated, 'God made this for a house of leisure', seem quite an appropriate one.

The Mansion

The mansion must have looked very different in, say, Queen Elizabeth's day. Fancy it without the noble front towards Finstock standing so proudly erect, its very appearance making simple folk afraid, and filling cottage people with awe.

All beholders know this is no common dwelling, the noble and the great must be here, it seems to say. The Forest front looks homely and comfortable; here could be happy, peaceful, domestic life; little children could have their toys, and romp and play. Bridget Ireton could read with wet eyes, and understanding let us believe, her father's letter, and stroll out here with it in her hand, praying as he wished her to do (strong, resolute man as he was) for him in his difficult task, unsought, but from which he felt he must not flinch.

At the corner there is Leicester's room.

Amongst the host of owners, occupiers, bailiffs, rangers of Cornbury and Wychwood, down the long years, very much could be said about them. I will give some particulars, which may be of interest, of a few about whom I know there is some local curiosity.

ROBERT DUDLEY

Robert Dudley, Earl of Leicester, had charge of Cornbury for a relative, Sir Henry Unton's widow, who was left with seven children. He seems to have used it as if it was his own. He does not appear to have been lacking in assurance, even if without some far more desirable virtues or qualities. He married in 1550 Amy Robsart before she was 20, and after she was found at Cumnor Place one Sunday night at the stair's foot dead (whispers pretty loud as to how she had got there were uttered, they are heard to-day) he aspired to the hand of Queen Elizabeth, whose favour he had won by his appearance and manners.

Once he was a prisoner, under sentence of death, within the Tower for trying to help get his kinswoman, Lady Jane Dudley, upon the English throne, but his neck was spared. The details of his life are not nice reading. I am glad many a cottage home about Cornbury could have given him a pattern of clean thought and life. But when at the end, at Cornbury, he climbed the stairs to his room after supper with Lettice Knollys, he was gone to his account before morning. Whispers about his death, too.

I do not like recording these dark pages, but there is dark and light in a true picture, and I am thankful there is more light than dark at Cornbury.

HENRY DANVERS

Henry Danvers had Cornbury given to him by King Charles I with Littleham meadow at Charlbury 'for ever'. He was the capable son of a clever and beautiful mother. In his early manhood he shared in a feud at Corsham, and it looks as if in a general scramble pistols were fired, someone was killed. So Henry felt it was safest on the far side of the English Channel till things were blown over a little, when amid the ringing of peals of bells he came home again. Filling posts of responsibility and honour he seems to have well filled his pockets, and coming to Cornbury he kept pretty well open house, and 'made money fly'.

In 1631 Nicholas Stone, mason and architect, built the south western wing at Cornbury, and also the fine gateway to the Botanical Gardens at Oxford. These gardens Danvers gave to the University, and they remain a beautiful retreat where all may go and enjoy the curious and wonderful plants cultivated there. He died January 20th, 1644, at Cornbury, aged 70, 'full of honour, woundes and daies,' so his monument records.

THE GREAT REBELLION

During the Civil War General Fairfax with troops was at Cornbury, also General Ireton with his newly wedded wife, Bridget Cromwell, who was 22. Carlyle says some interesting things about him, and gives the following letter Cromwell sent to his wife.

It is not considered just the thing to say anything in Cromwell's favour to-day perhaps, but it is well for those who can follow experimentally what this letter contains, to follow him to the deep places, and the heights he speaks of.

(Copy).

'For my beloved Daughter, Bridget Ireton, at Cornbury, the General's Quarters: These.

London 25 October 1646.

Dear Daughter

I write not to thy husband; partly to avoid trouble, for one line of mine begets many of his, which I doubt makes him sit up too late; partly because I am myself indisposed at this time, having some other considerations. Your friends at Ely are well: your Sister Claypole, I trust in mercy, exercised with some perplexing thoughts. She sees her own vanity and carnal mind: bewailing it; she seeks after (as I hope also) what will satisfy. And thus to be a seeker is to be the best sect next to a finder; and such an one shall every faithful humble seeker be at the end. Happy seeker, happy finder! Whoever tasted that the Lord is gracious, without some sense of self, vanity and badness? Whoever tasted that graciousness of His, and could go less in desire, — less than pressing after full enjoyment? Dear heart press on; let not Husband, let not anything cool thy affections after Christ. I hope he will be an occasion to inflame them. That which is best worthy of love in thy Husband is that of the image of Christ he bears. Look on that, and love it best, and all the rest for that. I pray for thee and him; do so for me.

My service and dear affections to the General and Generaless. I hear she is very kind to thee; it adds to my obligations. I am

Thy dear Father

OLIVER CROMWELL

Cromwell arranged for £700 to be spent on the forest walls, and that the deer were to have more care.

EDWARD HYDE

At the Restoration Charles II saw that his companion in exile, Edward Hyde, Earl of Clarendon, got Cornbury. His portrait is very like John Bunyan's. He built the striking east wing to Cornbury with its pilasters, pediment and arresting motto: DEVS NOBIS HAEC OTIA FECIT.

Hugh May designed; Thos. Strong, a local mason, carried out the work from stone quarried near at hand in the forest, no doubt using after the quarry sap had dried out. 'Dig one year, use the next,' is the old rule, or else the frost will play havoc with it.

It is said Clarendon failed once to have a proper dinner ready when King Charles rode over from Oxford. I dare say something was found, not 'bread and pull it.' It was said of Clarendon what certainly any man would rejoice to deserve:— 'A true Englishman, and certainly a very incorrupt man.'

His daughter, Anne, became the wife of James, Duke of York, 1660, later on King James II. Their daughter, Mary, became the wife of the Prince of Orange; whilst Anne, another daughter, became Queen Anne.

Part of the attendants of the Duchess and her three children in 1669 were: Mrs. Mary Roche (starcher) at £120 a year, a shoemaker at £36 10s., two (Sedan) chairman each £36, and three rockers £70 each.

THE PRETENDER

James, the reputed son of James Francis Edward, tried to get to the throne of England and is known as 'The Old Pretender'. His son, Charles Edward, supporting his father's claims (Bonnie Prince Charlie) is said to have been entertained at Cornbury in 1745. The Scotch firs above Charlbury station up Forest Lane are said to have been planted in his honour.

I have a fine bronze medal. Carolus III 1720 Rex 1766, with portrait. On reverse side: Ludouica Regina 1772 with portrait.

THE SPENCER FAMILY

Cornbury was purchased in 1751 by Charles, Duke of Marlborough, for his heir George, Marquis of Blandford, and later was called Blandford Park. Fortunately this name did not stick, and the old name prevailed.

Charles Somerset, Duke of Beaufort, lived there for many years, having hounds at Cornbury kennels. A memorial in Charlbury Church records the names of some of this family.

It eventually came to Francis George Spencer in 1845, whose wife, Lady Jane, was for so long Maid of Honour and friend of Queen Victoria, who at

Lord Churchill's death visited Lady Churchill here.

Lady Churchill was always kind to my grandmother, used to call and chat with her; and on her last visit wished to see me. As I was not at hand, she said 'Tell him to come up to Cornbury,' at a time she mentioned. On mother saying 'he will be afraid,' she said 'Why? There are no wild beasts up there.' When I arrived I was shown into the hall and had to wait some time. A kind old man came and said, 'Should you like a drop of beer?' This I declined. Presently I was taken before her Ladyship, and after she had looked at me, asking me questions, I answered to the best of my ability, was dismissed with a present for grand-mother. This I think was the last time I saw Lady Churchill. Question you are asking: 'Why did she want to see and talk with a Finstock village boy?' I cannot say. I never saw Lady Churchill but that she was wearing earrings made like little black tea kettles.

A Visit from the King and Bishop to the Wychwood Country

Our neighbourhood had a visit from King Richard II and the Bishop in 1390. They were both entertained at Eynsham Abbey. This was an expensive honour, and much money was spent upon it. The Bishop had a fee of £10, his clerk, his nine squires, thirteen valets, three grooms, and others all had presents. A pipe of wine was bought at Oxford.

Alano Fays collected dues from Cherelebery, Chadlington, Spellesbury, and Coate, assisted by Wm. Pomery, Beadle. Lauretino Peper saw that Faulore paid its share. Our manor, Childestone, Fynstock, etc., produced 6s. 8d. towards the big outlay of 'necersarii', namely: — linen, pewter, earthenware, canevas for the kitchen window, thread, wax, locks, keys, an axe; repairs to the bakehouse, farm and carpenters' tools, parchment, boots, saddlery, and candles. Building was repaired at Charlbury, whilst one John of Spellesbury, like another John, prepared the way, by road mending at a cost of xviiis. viiid.

The inner man was by no means forgotten. 'Salt fish, pickerells, red herrings, stock fish, 'aaburdener', cows, pigs, salmon, rabbits, oatmeal, vinegar, green peas, eggs, part of a 'lupus aquaticus', 1 lb. pepper from Stoke. Clothing and material, also a comb.'

So the king and bishop were prepared for, but the next item is, I think, most interesting. A layman, William Burden, was employed to paint an altar piece for which he was paid 6s. 8d. Is this the artist whose work is in our group of churches about Wychwood forest and in the cottage bedroom at Taston my father saw ?

When at this great visit of king and bishop, our local gentry, lay and clerical, were at the Abbey, the new picture would be sure to be one of the sights, and one can fancy the painter with his good old Wychwood name of Burden, would soon be booked up to paint pictures at Southleigh and our other churches. We will not forget his name, and our manor of Charlbury and hamlets produced his fee of 6s. 8d. for the Abbey altar piece.

Shorthampton

The wall paintings at this church, St. Frideswide teaching a child, St. Eligial the blacksmith, and other subjects discovered in 1903-4 are of interest. St. Sitha (see Frontispiece) is unique as a wall painting.

St. Sytha. Sitha. Citha, etc.

The following appeared in the *'Times'* newspaper last year, 1927.

I am perhaps the only living person who has unearthed a painting of this saint in an English church. This painting was found by me with many others of various dates in 1903-4 in the little hamlet chapel attached to the parish of Charlbury, Oxfordshire.

St. Sita appears on the wide flat hollows of a suite of mouldings to a large 15th century window in the south wall. She is painted against a red ground, bordered with amber; below the figure the ground was changed to black. She has a ringed and rayed nimbus of orange; on her head is a white kerchief or hood, with scarlet threads round the hem, and this appears to be pinned to a starched gorget or wimple, pleated under the chin. The lips are touched in with bright scarlet, otherwise the face is left white, and all the outlines are in black. Sita wears a white gown with surplice sleeves, and an emerald green mantle fastened by a bronze brooch. On her feet are little black shoes, and she bears in her hand two large metal purse frames, four substantial house-keeping keys, and a bag, perhaps containing broken meats for the poor — for Sita was both Martha and Mary — full of zeal in all practical charity and a pattern to the devout. The colours were extraordinarily brilliant when first released from the whitewash.

PHILIP M. JOHNSON, F.S.A.

See also the *Journal of the Royal Archaeological Institute*, 1905 (Vol. LXIII.)

The Black Death

In 1349 this terrible scourge swept the land, and so many people were carried off that there were not men enough to till the land; so much of the poorest land went out of cultivation, and this explains perhaps why in the fields there are parts that it can be plainly seen from the 'lands' and fences have at some time been arable, but so long ago that it is now permanent grass; some not far from where I write.

Land, rough pasture, was let at a penny per acre as the result, but meadow land was worth 4s. or 5s. an acre; and Charlbury meadow pasture went up to 8s. 8d. per acre.

In 1354 the Abbey dues were collected from Charlbury, Coate, Fawler, Fynstock; but Chilson, Thurme (where is this?), Walcote, Shorthampton, Chadlington were on lease, and Robert Langele gave to the bailiff 6 quarters wheat, 6 quarters argetum; Chadlington 31½ quarters wheat, 27 quarters dragetum, 12 of pulse.

Not a bad return was it so soon after the terrible pestilence. If all the Abbey property paid up as well as ours the monks held a special harvest thanksgiving service I should think.

In 1457 John Waver leased Walcot and Shorthampton tithes, the wheat fetched 5s. 6d. quarter, barley 1s. 2d. only.

John Purdy paid £7 for the tithes of Fawler in 1469.

Forest Fair

This famous fair was not of ancient origin as was Charlbury fair and market, which was granted February 7, 1256, by King Henry III, who was at Woodstock. 'Charlbury to have a market every Monday and a yearly fair to last four days, beginning on the feast of Assumption, August 14, and the three following days.' The king usually sent his glove, which was hoisted upon a pole as a signal that the fair was to begin; as is done at Exeter to this day. No doubt our town felt a thrill when the king's glove was put up at the top of Church Street in 1256, August 14.

About Forest Fair there is, I know, great interest and curiosity; its vast concourse of people, the wonders to be seen there, stories and traditions as to its size, and sad to say, its wickedness.

Portrait of Reuben Stratford cut at Forest Fair

The silhouette of my uncle, Rueben Stratford, was I understand cut there by some artist of the scissors and black paper for 1s. [See opposite.]

My father spent a never-to-be-forgotten night there as guard over a booth, to see all was safe. The sounds he heard around him, the cries, etc., of the scum left over by drink and sin when the respectable and more decorous part of the vast concourse had gone, were, I know, a recollection that moved and stirred him at their mention.

I know the fair was a horror to some, and strangely enough was unintentionally started, as described later, by a few godly people who wished to avoid Witney Feast influences.

The late Mr. George J. Jones, J.P., told me that his parents used to keep him and the other children locked in the house at Forest Fair, so great was their abhorrence of it and fearful that the children should get its influences in any way. *Jackson's Oxford Journal*, September 17, 1819, reports:

The annual Fair of Wychwood Forest was holden on Wednesday last. The unclouded and brilliant and sunny morning attracted a vast concourse of persons.

There was a down pour of rain later on, and it drove the pleasure folk helter skelter.

The late Mr. Jesse Clifford wrote the following:

The Forest Fair, albeit not strictly Charlburian, was practically so, for, being within 1½ miles of Newal Plain, in the forest, where it was held, and no other town near (Witney was five miles off) that could accommodate man and beast, Charlbury was full of parties, who for business or pleasure, came to the rendezvous from the Monday to the Friday of the week in which it was held on the Wednesday and Thursday. When in the heyday of its splendour and sin, Forest Fair was a sight once seen never to be forgotten. On the top and back of the plain near to the trees and bushes, stood the menageries of Wombell and Shore in full force of twenty or more carriages of beasts, etc., flanked at each end by smaller affairs, animals and human monstrosities such as the pig-faced lady and the calf with two heads, etc. I saw the seven-legged racer there. Boxing tents and theatricals, too, were there. About twenty yards in front of the shows was a street of booths for refreshments of both kinds, drink predominating. Another space, and on the brow of the hill overlooking the pond, was a well-planned street of stalls for sale of sweets and confectionery. Others, too, for sale of clothes, flannels, and hosiery. Pickled salmon was much patronised. The Vauxhall dancing saloon was there, with harps and violins, and when, at night, lit up with its 500 coloured lamps looked splendid. It had a buffet for the sale of refreshments, and retailed its famous sandwiches at 30s. per lb.

The gates of Cornbury Park (then Blandford Park) are thrown open for all carriages, carts, and vehicles carrying pleasure parties. The shows go up Burford Road, and by Ranger's Lodge, or come in from Witney. Passing through the Park you enter the forest at Buckleap Gate in the Vista Light, and on your right are a row of horses tethered to ropes secured to the trees; on the left hand carts, etc., under the care of the horse-keepers. The broad light is full of pleasure seekers wending their way to the plain. You reach it about two o'clock, and what a sight! There cannot be less than 15,000 to 20,000 in the tumultous sea of human beings. The plain is literally thronged, the shouting, the calling, the gongs, the music, is bewildering. On the lake you see Lord Churchill's pleasure boat (the *Fanny*), anchored at the upper end. Everybody seems bent on enjoyment. Lord Churchill, the Forest Ranger, has had the forest keepers and several of his workmen sworn in as special constables to preserve the peace. Hey! but it is a pleasant scene. But three o'clock has come, and a loud shout from Vista Light is heard. It is taken up by a crowd of sightseers, a lane is formed in front of the shows, and amid hurrahs and notes of welcome the carriage and four, with two postillions in scarlet and gold, of the Duke of Marlborough with the Duchess and family, followed by Lord Churchill's equipage, with coachmen and footmen in scarlet coats, red plush breeches, white stockings, and cockades. Then came B. Holloway, Esq., of Lee Place, and a long string of carriages of all the nobility and gentry round. These came back in the same order between booths and stalls. And now music is heard from the lake; on the boat is the Yeomanry Band, and martial strains mingle with the sounds on the plain.

'Tis tea-time now, and numerous little fires among the bushes tell you that parties are picnicing and enjoying the day in a rational manner.

You have seen the bright side of Forest Fair. Now for the reverse. Every kind of evil genius went there; thieves and pickpockets were in strong force. Rough and ready was the law enforced on the plain. I saw a pickpocket who had been detected, hustled down to the bank and ducked three times till nearly dead, he lay on the bank the very personification of abject despair. At the last fair held on the plain two Charlburians watched the manoeuvres of a woman with drunken men after the darkness set in. They kept her in sight, and she, noticing their espionage, came with an accomplice off for Charlbury. But just at the top of Watt's Lake Hill these two seized them, and out of her long hair they took seven watches, which they called their own. Lord Churchill had so many cases before him next day to adjudicate, that he limited the fair to one day, and eventually prohibited it on account of the drunkenness and debauchery, after existing for fifty years under different phases and conditions.

ORIGINATED IN METHODISM

A gentleman I knew well told me the origin of that famous holiday. He (Mr. Payne, of Fawler Mill) with Mr. Bolton, of Finstock, being well-known Wesleyans, with Mr. Early of Witney, agreed to invite their Methodist friends of Witney, Finstock, Charlbury, etc., to a picnic on the plain, on the Wednesday in Witney wake week, which was then the great day of the carnival, and so enjoy themselves without the fear of pollution. So successful was the affair that the third year a speculator, without their cognisance, brought refreshments, and so the thing increased, and about 1830 it reached its highest pitch of notoriety, and consequently of sin.

The Flora of the Wychwood Country

The flowers of the field abound in bewildering profusion and variety. The different conditions of soil and aspect, hill and dale make conditions favourable for a very extensive range of plant life.

Wychwood Forest and Cornbury Park, with Ditchley and other woods, our large extent of meadow land by the sluggish Evenlode here and the brisk sparkling Windrush yonder, with all the streams between, make a veritable paradise for wild flowers and plants, some rarities.

In spring the meadows, fields, hedgerows and woods are gay with primroses, followed in places with bluebells like a carpet. Violets grow in profusion, and white and yellow bedstraw covers many a margin of ditch and path. Wild roses are everywhere in variety and abundance. The meadow saffron abounds along the commons way, but I am not telling where rare and curious specimens of plant life are to be found, lest someone should go and destroy them.

If you see a plant or flower you have not seen before, do not gather it, let our Wychwood botanist know of it, Mr. W. H. Powell, who has done much as schoolmaster at Finstock for so long and, with his many articles in the Press, to foster the care and love of our local flora.

The deadly, the enchanter's and woody nightshades are here. Another poisonous plant, Henbane, used to grow on the Well Hill, Finstock, when I was a boy. It is but seldom found here now.

Birds

Our Wychwood birds deserve a better pen than mine to write about them. The first time I heard a nightingale, to know its song, I was with my father; he told me what it was. We could not see it — the thorns hid it — only the

'Jugjugjugjug' of the wondrous song could we hear. It used to sing most gloriously here at Charlbury, but has ceased to do so the last few years. Why is this? Never to be forgotten is the song of the skylark, as soaring away skywards at Finstock I first heard its song, to which the words seem to fit:—

'Up in a lift we go, te-hee, te-hee, te-hee, te-hee;

There's no cobbler on the earth can make a shoe to me

Why so? Why so? Why so? Because my heel's as long as my toe,' etc. etc.

The heron visits our meadows, and the green woodpecker comes from Cornbury into the orchard here. We hear and see it now and then. Its local name is 'He cul'. I have lively recollections of hearing an old forest keeper, when I was a boy, describe the flight of a carrion crow, but have not seen one to know it. The long-tailed tit is named by us 'Bum Barrel'. The gold-crested wren is hard to see. I never caught sight of one as a lad, and was ever on the look-out at Finstock.

Wychwood Beasts

The wolf and the boar have gone long ago, the badger has been more recent. The otter is with us, though I have never had a sight in our streams of this interesting, curious little beast that dogs and men spend precious time in hunting and trying to destroy — a pity. Against my will I have helped Reynard the fox to supply his larder. I only wish he could get his dinner as cheaply as he is said to rid himself of fleas. He takes a tuft of sheeps' wool into his mouth and wades into a pond, holding his nose aloft, till at last only the wool and the tip of his nose are above water. He waits till the livestock have all travelled to the bit of wool when suddenly he lets go of the wool and its cargo of undesirables, and the thing is done — so it is said.

Wychwood Oak

The quality of our timber was well known. There are records of grants of beams to buildings at Oxford, etc., and of course for ships it was very famous. Philip II of Spain told the commander of the Armada, so it is said, to bring back oak from Wychwood Forest. It is yet told how not only did our Mr. Gatfield serve under Nelson, but that the ship *Victory* was built from oaks felled on Charlbury Commons.

A kinsman of Robert Spendlove, the late Robert Heydon Gayner, had two ships built, with Oxfordshire names, *The Windrush*, and *The Wychwood*. After many voyages to South America and Australia *The Windrush* was reported sunk in collision with a Spanish ship a thousand miles off Sandy Hook. *The Wychwood* made many voyages to South America round Cape Horn, and was at last broken up. It is pleasant to think how, inland as we are, we are connected with 'those that go down to the sea in ships' and share in the business of 'great waters'.

A poor sailor asking a parish clerk for relief was told: 'You do not belong to our parish, so I cannot relieve you.' 'Sir,' replied Jack, with a big air, 'I lost my leg fighting for all the parishes in England.'

The fact of Sir Anthony Jenkinson, sea captain and traveller-ambassador, being in our parish accounts for two of the corbel heads in Charbury Church being sailors, no doubt.

CHARCOAL BURNING

Much charcoal has been burnt in Wychwood, and at one period it was forbidden to use any cleft wood, only round sticks, other oak being wanted for naval purposes.

The New Moon

Much superstition, hard to break away from, lingers about the appearance of the new moon. It clings to all our forest borders and far beyond.

To see it through glass the first time is unfortunate. Money must be turned. Lambs' tails must only be cut as ruled by the moon, even ladies' hair must be trimmed according to its position as rising, etc.

A few years ago, when waiting one night at a nearby railway station, the new moon, so fair and beautiful, came into sight, and a woman spoke across to the opposite platform to a friend, saying: 'Grannie always curtsies three times to the new moon.' Here, I thought, is a relic yet persisting amongst us from far-away days of 'bowing to the moon'.

The Sabbath

All round Wychwood was the belief that Sunday work and games led to disaster. The present generation seem to know it not, but it had a most restraining effect and tended much towards a quiet, peaceful day of rest and worship.

I remember a man saying he had noticed that if ever he had started off for a fair with his stall on a Sunday something was sure to happen. One instance he gave of how the spring of the cart snapped. Another man who went into the forest nutting on Sunday found the boughs brought down to his reach pretty easily, till he found to his alarm there was a cloven hoof in the bush, and he fled for home, a guilty, terrified man, to be ill for weeks before he recovered and was able to work, it is said.

Telling the Bees

Sugar did not come into use till after the Crusades; bees were extensively kept. Gold must be paid for a lot, then on setting them up in your garden, a woman told me, 'They must be told at night, "You have got a new master."' It was best to tell them of any death or change in the family. It was usual to tap the hives at nightfall and tell them.

Remedies, Touching &c.

Some of the old remedies are unprintable; many were most repulsive and nasty to use or take. A toad dried and hung round the neck, or put into a child's mouth, or slugs swallowed whole, give one a shock to think about.

Broth made from a fox, or oil from the same, was good for the gout, and the animal's blood was drunk as a remedy for the stone.

Grease from a roasted hedgehog was fine — so I have heard — for some complaints.

When sugar came to this land after the Crusades, treacle had a great fame for centuries as a remedy. The Bishops' Bible has 'Is there no treacle in Gilead?' (Jer. VIII., 22), using the word in the sense as understood in 1568 as a curative agent — hence the 'Treacle Bible'.

To cure a cold

I learnt as a lad a remedy for a cold:—
'Put your feet in hot water as high as your thighs,
Wrapp your head up in a flanelle as low as your eyes;
Take a quart of rumm'd gruele when in bed as a dose;
With a number four dippe well tallow your nose.'
Put the rum into the water for the feet — do *not* drink that.

The royal touch

Scrofula, or King's Evil, as it was called, could be cured by a royal touch. I heard of this when a lad, and later got two of the gold medal-like touch pieces given by King Charles II, who after prayers and psalms by the clergy, touched between the years 1660 and 1682 some 92,107 cases, giving to each person a gold touch piece.

An advertisement in *Jackson's Oxford Journal*, February 11th, 1758, is curious reading: —

> I George Kidler near Stroud in the County of Gloster, Broadweaver, at the desier of peepel hereabout, do give noutis that I have inockilated for these too seazons past between 2 and 300 for the Small Pox, and but too or three of them died ... I will God willing undertake to inockilate them for half a crown a head. Poor folk at a shilling a head.

The Radcliffe Infirmary

One could not live for long in one of our forest villages without hearing of 'The Infirmary', as it was called, at Oxford. From my earliest days I was hearing of this wonderful place and institution, and of the curious old chap in front, blowing the water skywards up through the shell he was holding. And then one and another went for treatment, and 'turns' — mysterious word to my young mind — were talked about, obtained, and used, all helping to turn one's thoughts that way.

We are told that Henry III in 1233, 'being touched with the Holy Ghost and moved with a regard to pity, ordained a certain famous hospital at Oxon, that therein infirm people and strangers might receive health and remedy of their health and necessity.' So he re-founded the Hospital of St. John.

It is a long jump from his day to 1758, when it is announced that 'The Radcliffe Trustees have agreed to erect a County Hospital', and a good many thousands of pounds have since then been spent in building, furnishing and maintaining this noble institution which for so long has ministered to the sick and suffering in all our district.

The physicians and surgeons who have so ungrudgingly devoted their services to the relief of suffering humanity deserve all praise.

Someone once made a little rhyme bringing in famous names:—

Dr. Hussey — slow but sure;
Dr. Symonds — kill or cure;
Dr. Hester — good old man —
Is sure to cure you if he can.

I have heard patients speak of the abundance of fresh air in the wards to-day, but when the first building was erected the upper window sashes were fixed and could not be lowered. When a movement was on foot to alter this some of the doctors objected. We move along, certainly.

The beds used to be filled with straw.

For long years each patient was allowed a pint and a half of beer a day. The nurses used to be paid £5 per annum; they were looked upon as servants. The first four engaged were 'to behave with tenderness to the patients, and with civility and respect to strangers'. In 1793 one nurse was known to have brought 'two bottles of ale to some of the patients'.

In 1847 the Board suggested that four shillings weekly be allowed one aged person on her retirement, she being nearly 75 years of age.

The institution deserves all support, and amongst novel and yet most effective means to help it, I would mention the Easter Egg Collection, originated in the practical brain of Councillor C. H. Brown. This has brought in a large number of eggs year by year, as well as cash from those who could not give eggs and yet wished to share in the good work.

Schools

Few people could write, even if they could read, in the Wychwood country not so very long ago. Very many had to use a mark, or X, and another person wrote their names, when signatures had to be made. Merchants and large traders had a 'mark', which was put upon their trade utensils, on their rings, their tokens, their houses sometimes, and on their memorial brasses (as at Chipping Norton Church can be seen) after they were dead. Accounts were kept, from the Exchequer downwards, by 'tallies' — that is, a stick had notches cut into it, then it was split, and the two parties each kept one. At a settlement the two parts were brought together, to tally, the notches counted and never a figure made. The Oxford breweries in quite recent years kept to this old system of tallies. Some of these can be seen at the Ashmolean Museum.

Mr. Henry Hall knew a man who ran two farms, had a house built, and before he started for market someone used to tell him which were five, and which ten pound notes. He put fives in one breast pocket and tens in the opposite side, and went off to business and made money.

Any person who could write letters was an asset to our villages. My grandmother did this for neighbours. She had been to a good school as a girl.

HORN BOOKS

One adjunct to the teacher's art has disappeared — the 'Horn Book'. This used to be put into the hands of every child who was fortunate enough to get any schooling, and school accounts show how great a number must have been in use. The 'book' was an oblong bit of board cut with a short projection at one end for a handle, the whole thing about perhaps five inches by three. On one side a sheet of transparent horn was held in position by some strips of thin brass round its edge, fastened with a few iron nails, covering a piece of paper that had upon it the alphabet, the vowels, and the Lord's Prayer, the whole prefaced by a small cross at the top right hand corner — hence 'criss cross row'. There is one at the Ashmolean, and, I believe, three at the Bodleian at Oxford. I think one turned up some years ago at Churchill from some cranny somewhere.

Sand spread on tables was used so that the children could write in it.

Quills, as the Charlbury school accounts show, were used for pen making in days quite near to ours, and when the map of Finstock parish was made the man who did this stayed at my grandfather's while engaged on the work, and on the floor of the middle bedroom in the Crown Inn he stretched his cloth, cutting his pens from crow quills. My father, then a boy, ground his ink for him in the bottoms of turned-up tea saucers.

Blotting paper had not come into use, and fine sand (see Charlbury school accounts) was sprinkled over writing from a 'pounce box', something like a wooden pepper box.

And yet what splendid penmanship they turned out! Old account books show this. Schoolmasters put fine work into inscribing their pupils' names in their summing books. My father's book was embellished by the Grammar School master here, and he did it with his left hand, his right arm being withered and hanging at his side.

The Quakers had schools at Charlbury, Burford, and Witney.

I am glad to be able to give some particulars of the 'Charlbury Grammar', 'Gatfield's' and 'British' schools, to which for generations the Wychwood district sent pupils.

Charlbury Grammar School

A document in the church chest at Bampton, dated October 10th, 1653, re the appointment of the first school-master at that place, reads:—

'Now know ye that ... Wm. Hodges, William Veysey, Thos. Willer and Wm. Hancks have elected placed and appointed William Jackson M.A. of Charlbury.'

In the light of this and the extract from Mrs. Anne Walker's will, which follows, Wm. Jackson, M.A., went to an endowed school that guaranteed a salary, leaving Charlbury, which was unendowed.

Good Anne Walker saw that this was altered, as follows:

Mrs. Anne Walker's will, proved 1667. Extract:

She bequeaths to Charlbury—

Which is great and full of poore inhabitants who by reason of their great poverty are not well able to maintayne and educate their children at school, whereby they are brought upp in ignorance and though there be in the said town house, or houses, sometimes used heretofore for a school house, yet for want of maintenance for an able schoolmaster to teach the School there, the same hath been for a long time disused and whereas (being desirous to promote the good of the said town and their poor children should be brought up in the fear of God and good literature) and minded in case the said town be at the charge to make the said house fit for a free school and for the habitation of an able schoolmaster and will appreciate and settle the same, to have perpetual continuance to such end and purpose to give and settle an annuity the rent 40£, etc, etc.

After Wm. Jackson had left in 1653 Moses Greenwood, M.A., of Brazen-nose College, had a school here, and though Ann Walker had left her bequest charged on her estate at Cropredy and Shotteswell in 1667, nothing seems to have been done till Charlbury sent a petition to the Governors of Brazen-nose College in 1675, asking that they appoint Moses Greenwood, M.A., as master of the Walker

School. Evidently the appointment was made. By the kindness of the authorities of the college I recently saw the petition (with other parchment deeds of the school) yet preserved in the college archives. The petition is as follows:—

PETITION FROM CHARLBURY TO BRASENOSE COLLEGE
December 10th, 1675.

Whereas Moses Greenwood Master of Arts formerly of Brazen-nose Colledge in Oxon hath for several yeares past been very careful and industrieus in the true instructing the youth of the Towne of Charlbury in the County of Oxon in Grammer-Learning, and is a person of unblameable conversation: it is the humble petition of us, whose names are underwritten, Inhabitants of the said Towne of Charlbury that the Principall and ffellowes of the said Colledge of Brazen-nose constituted Governors of the Schoole and Electers of the Schole-Master these, by the last will and Testmt. of Mrs. Walker the ffoundresse thereof, would nominate settle and confirm the said Mr. Greenwood Schoole-Master of the said place.

Thos. ffulks Vicar	ffrancis Pridie
George Tennant senr	George Tennant
Thomas Harris	William Willis x his mark
William Pridie	George Warde
George Tennant junr	Thomas Priddie x his mark
William Porter	John Coats senr
Edmund ffowler	John Coats junr
John Fowler	John Tennant
Alexander Allworth	John Hastings
Robert Larget	William Rosse x his mark
Robert Brookes	Thomas Sympson
ffrancis Atkinson	William Ryman
John Preddie	John Smith
	Thos. Marshall

STATUTES AND ORDINANCES OF THE WALKER SCHOOL
The statutes, ordinances, etc., of the school are on two sheets of parchment about two feet six inches by two feet, and were drawn up in 1675 by Richard Eyans, who was, I believe, Ann Walker's brother, and who had gone to live at Enstone, where several generations of his family lived in a mansion near the church, now destroyed. As will be seen from the extracts which follow he endeavoured to set forth in plain English with quaint spelling, what he considered the right lines on which the school should be conducted, but to-day they

are very interesting reading as to the management of a school, and modern educationalists will smile to read them:

Statutes Ordinances Orders and Directions made ordained appointed and established by Richard Eyans of Enstone late of Charlbury in the said County of Oxon Gent, to whom the power of makeing and ordaining such statues and ordinances descended and came as son and heir of Richard Eyans late of Charlbury ... Gent. deceased who had the same by right of Survivorship touching and conccrning the Government of the free Schoole in Charlbury aforesaid endowed by the last will and testament of Ann Walker late of the City of London deceased and touching and concerning the Election ordering direction or expulsion of the Schoole master of the said free schoole and of two exhibitioners to be chosen out of the s.d. free Schoole to be maintained in Brazen-nose Colledge in Oxon which are to be kept and observed for ever as followeth—

1. Imprimis it is hereby ordained and established that the Principall and scholers of the same Colledge and their successors shall choose one Godly diligent and able person out of the s.d. colledge if any may or can be found fitt to be Schoolemaster of Charlbury Schoole and so from time to time and at all times for ever hereafter and as often as the s.d. place of Schoolemaster shall hapen by death or other wise to be void within one month after the same shall so become void and that they the s.d. Principall and Scholers and their Successors shall (as visitors) of the s.d. schoole from time to time have and take upon them the oversight and see the ordering and Government of the s.d. Schoole according to the true intent and meaning of the said will.

3. Item it is further ordained according to the said will that they the said principle and Schololers and their Successors shall nominate and appoint out of the poorer sort of Scholers in the said Colledge two most eminent in their Judgement for piety and parts to receive and enjoy an annuity or exhibition of five pounds a year a piece until such scholers shall respectively have taken the Degree of Master of Arts or shall be of Competent standing in the said University to take the s.d. Degree and no longer, and so from time to time for ever and that they shall and will in all their Elections prefer such poor Scholers as have been bred up in or come from the s.d. schoole to the s.d. Colledge (if any be fitt) or in default thereof shall nextly prefer such poor scholers as were born in the County of Oxon.

6. Item it is ordained that the Schoole Master shall be ready with his scholers in the Schoole every morning in every week in the year from the

tenth day of March to the 10th day of September at Six of the Clock in the morning there to continue till eleven, and at one in the afternoon there to continue till five in the evening, these last rules and orders tuching and concerning the coming to, and continuing at, and departing from the Schoole to be for ever duely kept and observed save only upon Holy Days, Saturdays in the afternoon and Thursdays at three of the Clock in the afternoon and the usual times allowed to Scholars for Recreation and visiting their friends at the feast of Christmass Easter and Whitsuntide and at other times as are and shall be appointed by publique authority.

7. Item it is ordained that the Scholers shall have notice of the repairing to schoole by ringing of a bell at some meet space before the hours above specified when they ought to come by Some poor Scholer to be by the Master appointed from time to time for this purpose to ring the bell and to sweep the School who for that end shall have threepence a quarter geathered of every Scholer throughout the whole Schoole save only of such children of ye poorest inhabitants of the said town of Charlbury.

8. Item it is ordained that the Schoolmaster with his Scholers shall first every morning address themselves to God by prayer in the Schoole house by some ordinary prayers such as are set forth in the book of Common Prayer and of such other prayers as shall be found and prepared by the visitors for that purpose, and likewise before their dismission in the evening they shall close the day with prayer and thanksgiving and the Schoole master is hereby enjoyned to take care that these religious duties be dayly and diligently performed and attended by all the scholers.

9. Item it is ordained that the said Schoole shall be for ever free for the teaching the English Latin and Greek tongues to all such male children whose parents now do or hereafter shall Inhabitt the town of Charlbury with the children of ye aforesaid Richard Eyans, Party to these presents and Anthony Eyans his Brother and all the Children and issue males of them or any or either of them respect being stil had to the children of the poorest Inhabitants of the said town of Charlbury according to the last will and testament of Ann Walker deceased And all to be taught by the Schoole master freely without requiring anything for the same upon pain of expulsion for ever.

14. Item no Scholer shall at any time with knife or otherwise howsoever cut knotch deface or breake the windows, wainscotts, formes, seats, table of orders, deskes, doors or tables in any part of the Schoole or house, the Master upon conviction to give them exemplary punishment for deterring others so to do.

15. Item for the better encouragement of the Master of the said free schoole the Master is hereby priviledged to teach such a number of foreigners as the visitors shall think convenient and to make what agreement he pleaseth for teaching all such foreigners.

MASTERS

1675.—Moses Greenwood, M.A. He entered Brazen-nose at sixteen, and at his death, March 1st, 1679, he was buried in the College Cloisters.

1679.—Henry Allen. It appears from inscriptions on stones in the church floor that he married Elizabeth, daughter of Wm. Pridie, mercer. She died 1689, aged 28. A stone records Mary Allen, 1718, aged 15.

1731.—J. Arrowsmith. He signs the transcript of our parish registers now in the Bodleian as Curate here in 1740.

1761.—Jas. Williamson (Queen's College).

1787.—Richard Thorne. He also signs as Curate.

1792.—T. Oakley (resigned 25th March, 1833).

1835.—Jas. Crawford.

1835.—John Hills. Wrote with his left hand, but was a fine penman.

1849.—Thomas Lowder (conditionally appointed). Did he accept?

1850.—Henry Rowley.

1855.—George Morris.

WALKER SCHOLARS, THE FIRST FOUR

1675-6.—John Jackson, son of William of Northleach. Thomas Matthews, son of Timothy of Eynsham, admitted Brasenose 1675. M.A. 1681. Perhaps Vicar of Enderby with Weston, in Leicester.

1678.—James Croome, son of James of Malmesbury. M.A. 1685. Rector of Weston juxta Bath 1691, and of Newton St. Loe, Somerset.

1681.—Thomas Simpson, son of Thomas of Chester City. B.A. Hart Hall 1685. Scholar of Charlbury School.

Private Schools

From a letter written in 1798 by Mrs. Edens, of Honeybourne, who had been staying at her daughter's, Mrs. Jno. Payne's, at Fawler Mill, where had come a mob of five or six hundred strong, twenty or so armed with bludgeons, declaring they would pull the mill down to the ground. She says: 'Mary Nind and her sister thought of opening a school at Charlbury.' Twelve children were promised them, but as provisions were so dear and to board them out would cost 15/- a week the scheme seems to have been given up.

Later on Mr. Thomas Pentycross Gatfield, one of Nelson's seamen, came to his native place and opened a school which for many years was a success.

Fisher's Lane here was quite an educational centre in his day.

Prospectus of Mr. and Mrs. Gatfield's School:—

CHARLBURY SCHOOL

Mr. and Mrs. GATFIELD beg leave to present their most grateful acknowledgments to their friends, and respectfully inform them and the public, that their SCHOOL will re-open on Monday, 21st instant.

Terms

	£	s.	d.
Board and Education of Young Ladies Including English, Writing, and Accounts, Needlework, plain and ornamental	16	16	0
Entrance	0	10	6
Young Gentlemen under 12 years of Age, boarded, and taught Reading, Writing and Arithmetic	16	16	0
Twelve and upwards	18	18	0
Entrance	0	10	6

Charlbury British School, 1815

The account book begins 1817, and from that book and the earliest minute book I can discover, I gather that Robert Spendlove gave £100 to start the institution, a committee took it up and hired a room at the Bell Inn for meetings, got distinguished local gentry to take an interest, and occasionally had a dinner, the profit from which festive occasion is entered as 'over from dinner, £1 14s. 10¹/₂d.'

Many donations are recorded, quite small items some of them. The largest — two sums of £2 — were given by Lord Churchill and Edward Smith, in 1818. Many sums were lent to form a fund so that the building could be erected and the school opened, as it was in 1817.

The earliest list of officers and committee available is for the year 1826.

CHARLBURY BRITISH SCHOOL SOCIETY, 1826.
OFFICERS AND COMMITTEE.

Patrons:

The Duke of Beaufort.

The Earl of Normanton.

Patronesses:

The Duchess of Beaufort.

The Countess of Normanton.

President:

George Frederick Stratton, Esq.

Vice-President:

William Henry Ashton Smith, Esq.

Ladies' Committee:

R. Gibbons.

R. Albright.

H. Sessions.

E. Penson.

H. Albright.

M. Albright.

S Jones.

M. Sessions.

L. Sessions.

E. S. Bowls.

Mary Sessions.

Rachel Albright, *Secretary.*

General Committee:

Nicholas Albright.

Thomas Stow.

Robert Sessions.

Edward Kerby.

Ed. Walden.

William Jones.

Geo. Horniblow.

Jona. Paine

Wm. Padbury.

Wm. Albright, *Treasurer.*

Jas. Sessions, *Secretary.*

The British School, 1815

The old minute and account books of the British School record what are now curious and interesting items. Sand was used for drying writing, blotting paper not being in use; quills for pens, coins of light weight.

The scholars must attend church or some place of worship twice on the Lord's day, and it appears from the school accounts that a James Knibb went to see to those who went to church, being paid to do so, and from the number of entries 'Beer for Knibb, 3d.'; he found it a thirsty job. In 1822 it looks as if the windows got smashed: 'Glasiers bill, £1 9s. 10d.'

Dr. Silver, the Vicar, wanted the schoolroom to hold a Sunday school. The committee said he could have it on payment of 1s. per month, but they seem to have been rather uncertain as to what he was going to teach, so a deputation was to wait upon him, which they did, but he did not take on.

In 1830 a debt was still on the building, but Esquire Smith said he would give £60 if the remainder could be subscribed, and William Jones and his wife gave £10 and Nicholas Albright the remaining £15, and the school Robert Spendlove had given £100 to start was free of debt.

The salary paid the master was £40 per annum, or £20 and the pence, 'no child to pay more than one penny per week.' There were quite a number of masters in the early years of the school's history, and not all on the same terms. One master on leaving asked for the testimonials he brought, and they were refused him. The governess was paid in 1828 a salary of £7 4s. for the year. Children came in from the district round about. In 1828, out of a total of 157 there were 67 from Stonesfield and other places. No motor — only Shanks' pony then.

The schoolroom was granted for a temperance meeting in 1832.

Charles Leake, of Witney, gave £5 to the school in 1834. Thomas Dyke left a legacy of £5, and Richard Taylor, of Chilson, gave £5.

In 1839 the school was closed on May 28th and remained closed until October 10th, 1842, when Mr. Jesse Clifford was appointed master, and from that day, under his hand, till 1885 the school prospered, and in this land and overseas there are his scholars who 'rise up and call him blessed.'

From school accounts:—

'This book 2s. 6d.' ' Sand 3d., wafers 2d.' 'E. Seager one month's salary £3 6s. 8d.' 'Paid Betty Maycock for repairing cloaks 4/-.' ' Light gold 3/-.' ' Bad silver dollar 5/-.' 'Reading Thomas Dyke's will 1/-.' 'Beer to Welford &c. 5d.' 'Coal £3 1s., turnpikes 5/-, beer for carter 7d., unloading 1/6, attendance 4d.' 'Beer for Knibb's 3d.' 'Paid Thos. Welford 41 weeks at 7½d., £1 5s. 7½d.' 'Jas Knibbs attending the boys at church 4/4½, beer for Knibb 3d.' 'Jas Knibb two weeks 1/3.' 'Bottle wine 6/-.' '1 yard muslin for girls to learn to whip 1/6.' 'My Own £3 15s. 0d.' 'Pd. Jas. Knibb 29 weeks 18/11½. Beer to ditto 3 times 9d.' 'Knibbs attendance at church 10/-. Ditto for Xmas Day 7½d.' 'Shavings at different times 3d.' 'Jas. Knibbs 10 Times in church, Ash Wed. and Good Friday so called 6/5. Beer 3d.' ' Pd. for visitors book 3/6. Pd. for bell 4/-.' 'Bell and whistle 2/-.' 'Ink and Quills and Pencil 9½d. Blue Paper ½d.' 'Flour for paste 6d.' 'Hair cutting 1/5.' 'Soap 2d.' 'Rewards £4 1s. 1¾d.' 'Letter to London 9d.' 'Carriage of subscription from Mr. Smith 3d.' 'Breaking coal 6d.' 'Two new oak legs 1s. 9d.' 'Gratuity 2/6.' 'Thomas Kibble's work and stone 1/-.' 'Reward to Oxford Lad. Lad journey to and from Oxford 1/6.' 'Soap 1¾d.' 'Ink 2½d.' — this item often occurs. 'Ed. Kerby rent of room fire &c. £1 5s. 0d.' The committee met monthly at the Bell Inn. 6/- is entered for a bottle of wine.

The windows must have got broken pretty frequently, as there are often glaziers' charges entered.

'Chaise to Oxford £1 9s. 10.' No explanation who had this, or for what purpose.

Mr. Jesse Clifford made the ink used by the school in his day.

A statement at the end of one book shows that the building cost £245 4s. 10d., and including that item the cost to work the school for the first nineteen years was £1,700 8s. 9¾d. Some of the masters during that period had received the pence as part of their salary, so that is not included in the figure.

Masters' names gathered from the accounts:

E. Seager. Edward Hopkins. Napthali Phillips. Francis Thompson. Thomas Davis. Samuel P. Witt. James Dodwell. Chas. Brand. Mr. Jesse Clifford.

A List of Local Masters

A sixpenny reading book with no date gives the following:—

Recommendations.

We, whose names are hereunto subscribed, having perused a Manuscript, entitled Rusher's Reading made most Easy, do reccomend it as the most useful Book, for the Instruction of Children, in the rudimental parts of Reading

Thos. Stockley, Schoolmaster, in Banbury.

R. Grimbly,   ”   ”

I. Woolston, Boarding School, Adderbury.

Geo. Pitt Allen, Schoolmaster, Woodstock.

T. Richmond, Free School, Horley.

William Harris, Schoolmaster, Bloxham.

Thomas Thompson, Teacher of the Classics in Ledwell, Oxon.

John Carr, Schoolmaster, in Oxford.

James King   ”   ”

Joseph Bardgett   ”   ”

Richard Skillman, Teacher of the Mathematics in Deddington.

Thos. Tomalin, Schoolmaster, Byfield.

J. Biggers, Schoolmaster, Witney, Oxon.

Wm. Turner, Teacher of the Classics and Mathematics in Witney.

Thos. May, Schoolmaster in Witney.

Wm. Meads, Teacher of the Classics in Ensham, Oxon.

William Castle, Free-School, Ensham.

Richard Tennant, Schoolmaster, Enstone.

T. Bliss, Schoolmaster, Chipping Norton.

Edw. Banbury, Schoolmaster, Charlbury.

Finstock — Apprentices

Friendless children were put as apprentices to those considered able and qualified to take them, I believe whether they would or no, and here is given an indenture dated 1727, relating to Susanna Parslow being put with Elizabeth Holloway of Fawler:—

This Indenture witnesseth that Henry Lankford, overseer for the poor in the Town of ffinstock in the parish of Charlbury in the County of Oxon and Simon Birdseye Churchwarden of the same Town By and with the consent of Sir Robert Banks Jenkinson Bart. and Sir Jonathan Cope Two of His Majesties Justices of the Peace for this same county have placed and by these presents Do put place and bind Susanna Parslow being a poor fatherless and motherless Child as an apprentice to and with Elizabeth Holloway of ffawler in the Parish of Charlbury aforesaid, with she to dwell from the 29th of September last past for and during unto the full end and Term of five years (or be married which shall first happen) according to the statute in that case made and provided During which time and term the said Sussanna Parslow shall the said Elizabeth Holloway her Dame well and faithfully serve in all lawful Business as the said Sussanna Parslow shall be put unto according to her power will and honesty and obediently in all things shall behave her self towards the said Elizabeth Holloway and her children and family. AND the said Elizabeth Holloway for her part covenanteth promiseth and agreeth that for and in consideration that the said overseers and churchwardens have given and delivered unto she the said Susanna Parslow all these particular things of Apparel hereafter mentioned (that is to say) Six new Shifts, Six good Caps, four good handkerchiefs, Two good Linin Aprons, Two Woollen Aprons, Three pair of hose, Two new pair of Shoes and new pair of Pattens, Two new petty coats, one new Gound Two other good Gounds, Two other good petty coats, and one new Straw Hat. She the said Elizabeth Hollaway the said Sussanna Parslow in the art and skill of Housewifery in the best manner as may or can be shall teach and inform or Cause to be taught and informed much as thereunto belongeth and as she the said Elizabeth Holloway knoweth and also during the said term to find and allow unto her said apprentice sufficient meat drink, Linnen Woollen Shoes Stockings Washing Lodging and all other necessarys meet for such an Apprentice And also at the end of the said Term she shall find Elizabeth Holloway shall give and deliver unto her said apprentice as good and sufficient apprell as she came apprentice with. IN WITNESS whereof the parties above said to these proposed Indentures their hands and seals interchangeably have set the first day of the December in the fifth year of the Reign of our Sovereign Lord George the second by the Grace of God of Great Britain ffrance and Ireland King Defender of the Faith Anno Dom 1727.

ELIZABETH HOLLOWAY.

Sealed & delivered in
the presence of
WILLIAM HARRISON his mark X
GEORG NOBLE

RO. BANKS JENKINSON
JONA: COPE.

An Army Substitute from Finstock

When men were drawn for the army, if a substitute could be found and he was suitable, he went instead. Below is an old document relating to this:—

OXFORD REGIMENT OF MILITIA

This is to certify that Jesse Turner Private was on 18th March 1803 sworn in, and enrolled to serve in the Oxford Militia as a substitute for Wm. Smith of the Parish of Witney in the County of Oxford and that the said Jesse Turner is now actually serving in a Detachment of the above Regiment under my command at

Given under my hand at

Head Quarters

22nd Nov. 1813

ROBERT SISPIONTION

Major Commᵈ Batt.

Detachment.

To whom
it may concern.

The Flail

'Two sticks a leather and thong,
    Will tire a man, let him be ever so strong.'

Formerly all corn was thrashed out by the flail on wood floors so constructed that the spring of the floor met the flail, so preventing the corn being bruised between them. I have watched this as a lad, standing outside the 'cratch', as the low door which kept the corn from bouncing out into the yard was called. Jimmy Lowe, at Finstock, used to thrash out the small lots of barley, etc., grown on the allotments.

Long ago my grandfather suggested to Lord Churchill what a boon it would be if he let the field near where now is the church, in allotments, and it was done.

When talking near the gate one day his lordship said, 'A very nice smell about here.' When he had ridden away an enquiry at the corner cottage elicited, 'Yes, we are just cooking a couple of bloaters for dinner.'

I saw a horse thrashing machine in use, and a local genius had made a machine, as recorded by some rhymster:

'Frankie Benard, the pride of the green,
    With his wheelbarrow, truck, and thrashing machine.'

The curious old canvas flip flap for winnowing corn I saw used a little.

The Curse

'When I remember I am afraid.' — Job.

The belief in the withering and blighting effects of an evil deed, especially if a curse or denunciation was uttered by the injured party, lingers yet amongst us.

St. Frideswide 1,200 years ago, hidden amongst the pigs at Bampton in the Bush, put a curse on all kings who should visit Oxford. She was pursued by her royal lover. Unfortunate things did happen to several — Charles I, who resided there for some time, is a conspicuous example.

A poor girl at Spelsbury, long ago, had read over her grave one of the denunciatory Psalms. Just turn up the hundred and ninth — one would not care to be the person cursed by its terrible words. Evil pursued those who oppressed the poor and helpless. I have witnessed happenings reminding one of a page from the Old Testament — some which cannot be recorded — so surely has disaster and even death followed sin. In slow village life we saw, felt, witnessed with silent wonder sins visited even upon the children. In some cases a whole family wiped out and gone.

'They that plow iniquity, and sow wickedness, reap the same ... by the breath of His nostrils are they consumed.' *(Eliphaz)* — *Job.*

Marriage Customs, etc.

Interest has always centred round the marriage ceremony, the oldest institution of society, and about which are some of our most ancient customs and laws.

It has been said, and the view is yet held by many, that it is a sacrament. Calvin declared it to be an institution of God.

Our Anglo-Saxon forefathers were met at the Church porch by the priest, who there blessed the ring and gave it to the bridegroom, who placed it on the middle finger of the the bride's left hand. They were then led into the church. The priest at some places twisted his stole round the joined hands of the couple at the words, 'These whom God hath joined together,' hence the saying about our forest borders, 'Tying the knot.'

MARRIAGE SEASONS

I never heard or dreamt there was any season for these interesting and necessary events till, some years ago, I heard of someone not very far away who said 'she could not be married during Lent.' I find the Church used to be very strict about this, and an old almanac (1674) put it in black and white.

Times Prohibiting Marriage this year;

Marriage comes in on January 13th and at Septuagesima Sunday it is out again until Low Sunday, at which time it comes in again and goes not out till Rogation Sunday. Then it is forbidden till Trinity Sunday, from whence it is unforbidden till Advent Sunday, and then it goes out and comes not in again till the 13th January next following.

An old saying: 'Who marries between the sickle and the scythe, will not thrive.'

THE RING

Henry VIII gave Anne of Cleves a ring inscribed with the poesy: 'God send me well to keep,' and this custom of having something engraved around the inside of the ring used to be of pretty frequent occurrence. As mentioned in my *Notes on Charlbury*, more than one have turned up in the soil in this neighbourhood. In days past extreme poverty in our forest villages made marriage to many a difficult thing. The necessity for a ring was got over in some of our nearby churches by using the ring of the church door key. I could possibly have got further particulars of this from my grandmother Stratford whom I have heard speak of it. Rings were borrowed — my grandmother lent hers in order that one couple could be joined in marriage.

So limited were the means that in some cases, as in Bunyan's, only the barest necessities could be had. In a hamlet not far from where I write a couple got wed and children came, and all the cutlery they possessed was one knife. One day the children got this precious knife, took it out, and lost it. When dinner time came — it was on Sunday, too! — what was to be done to divide the food they had? At last the father said to his wife, 'Sally, go upstairs and fetch my raz-zur (razor) down.'

There was much joy and happiness in very bare little homes. Without the things seemingly so necessary to many now, our village fathers did nobly, and given health and food and shelter it was wonderful what pleasure and delight could be found in the simplest life. The mansion had its delights, no doubt, but so did the cottage. The good wife loved and was proud of her man, and if she lost him loved his memory still, even if she could not do as John de Balliol's widow, Devergoil, did, in the thirteenth century. She had her husband's heart 'embalmed in sweet-smelling spices and laid in a coffer of ivory ever by her side. Always, at meat the coffer was set at table, and she did reverence to it, as though he were present.'

WEDDING BELLS

The bride and groom we greet,
    In holy wedlock joined,
Our sounds are emblems sweet
    Of hearts in love combined. — 1786.

The above inscription is on a bell, and generally the bells ring out a merry clangour on the occasion of a wedding, the ringers getting a tip in recognition of their share in the joyful proceedings. At the villages where there are no bells all and sundry, equipped with horns and other noise-producing things such as villagers know of, assemble about the house at nightfall, only dispersing when toll was handed out to be divided amongst them.

THE SKIMMINGTON

Those who broke their marriage vows were treated to a horrible din of 'rough music', as it was called. Their neighbours assembled at night and showed disapproval by the blowing of horns and beating of tin cans. Sometimes effigies were made and burnt. This old way of holding transgressors up to shame was most effective, as to the village and immediate neighbourhood. The 'rough music' and din, with effigy burning, was quite the old way of showing public disapproval of anything that had been done, and no doubt even now could soon be called forth in our forest borders should public feeling demand it.

A Wychwood Love Story

A very charming old man I knew was as a youth employed as garden boy and footman by a gentleman who had, I think, an only daughter, and the following story I piece together from what I have gathered about them.

These young people naturally saw a good bit of each other, and presently the lad thought his young mistress was more than kind, and this he decided to test. When waiting at table his hand somehow touched hers, and when driving the gig he drove over rough ground, so there was a good deal of jolting, and presently they understood. Matters came to a climax after some time, for her father came on them suddenly in a summer house one day, and she was sitting—but not on the seat. After this they decided something must be done, and so agreed to do what is not the best or wisest thing, that was to run away and get married.

Plans were made. He was to bring a ladder to her window and she would be ready with her money and jewels, and they would walk to the city some miles away and be wed by special licence. The ladder was brought and the lady got out of the window and they got clear away, when they found that in the hurry and excitement she had left both purse and jewels on the bed in her room. This, however, was a trifle compared with the joy they felt was before them as they pressed on.

The ceremony was just concluded when the father of the lady, with officers of the law, appeared at the church door, and the youthful bridegroom soon found himself in the lock-up. Matters were not so easily settled, however, for the lady, with fine spirit declared that until her husband was released she would neither eat nor drink, and she did not.

After a time her friends came round, and they assisted the young folk to go into business. The husband became a useful member of the religious body to which he belonged. An old lady who in those early days lived near told me, 'She used to come to the village chapel carrying her baby, like the rest of the women, to the services.' A friend of mine had pleasant recollections of how kind she was to him when as a lad he lived near.

When I visit the village churchyard where rests till the great day the girl who gave up all for her lad, I like to read what he had put at the foot of the simple stone which marks her grave:

'She always made home happy.'

Epitaphia

'On a stone in Esqr. Holbridge's garden.' (MS. note of my grandfather's):—
'Here lie the Bones of a poor Thrush,
Whom Death alone did crush.
Before he was fledged young Henry caught him,
And to the cage he quickly brought him,
Where he with care and tenderness was fed,
But now, alas, poor Dickey's dead.
So must we wretched mortals die,
And in the dust like Dickey Lye.'
     — 'Wm. Kibble, May 21, 1809.'

Translation of epitaph formerly in Chantry Chapel, north side of Enstone Church:—

'Beneath this stone rest the bones of Richard Eyans, Gent., near the ashes of a most beloved wife, by whom he had two sons and four daughters, the most chaste pledges of his marriage couch, in whom they as if their own survivors yet live. Who having completed his forty-fourth year, fell into a fatal illness, which at this time being Epidemic they called Rheumatism, and, seized upon by the blind envy of death, who knows not how to spare even the most excellent, breathed out his soul October 3rd, 1677.'

At Spelsbury, on a headstone to Robert Mace, of Taston, clock-maker and blacksmith:——

'My sledge and hammer lie declined,
My bellows, too, have lost their wind,
My fire's extinct, my coal's decayed,
And in the dust my vice is laid;
My forge is left, my iron is gone,
My nails are drove, my work is done.'

The great snowstorm of 1881 is kept before us in an epitaph in Enstone churchyard. I look at it sometimes and think of the fearful snowstorm.

'In Memory of Henry Harling,
who perished near Deddington
in the great snowstorm,
January 18th, 1881.
Aged 33 years.
"Thy will be done." '

At Charlbury:——

'In Memory of RICHARD COOMBS, of Finstock, who was killed on October 2nd, 1851, aged 21 years, by a falling of earth in Sydenham Mead near this Church whilst cutting the hollow way for the Rail road.

'Fame sounds the soldier's praise
Who dies in victory or war,
Why should we not record the fall
Of those who died to serve us all,
In works that lead to love and peace,
Before whose power all wars shall cease.
More dear to man and nearer God
Is death in peace, than death in blood.
Then, blessings on the Rail man's tomb
And peace attend the soul of Coombs.'

At the bottom of this grave was found a Roman brooch. A lad noticed it and picked it up; he received a guinea for it. I heard it was at the British Museum, but on inquiry it could not be traced there, and it was suggested that it might be in the Ashmolean Museum, but there is no trace of it there.

Another stone reads:—

'In Memory of Mary wife of Isaac Mobbs who died Dec. ye 7th 1787, aged 47 years.

'Draw near to me my children dear,
      See where your mother lies:
Close in the dust until the day,
      Our bodies shall arise.
To part with you great grief it was
      More joys for to insue;
I hope for mercy in that day
      And there to meet with you.'

Epitaph at Tackley:—

        'Here lyeth ye bodies of
        Samuel & John Hodges
        who both died in the water togr
        Dec. 7th 1710. Samuel was
        31 years old John 26.
'Mourne not for we dear friends our Glass is run,
By Water we did loose our lives so soon,
So Nimbly came Death & took us out of hand,
And would not suffer us to set our foot on Land.
For it so pleased God in the prime time of our years
To take our Souls from all these worldly cares.'

On a small headstone of chaste design without any name and date, also at Tackley, in capitals:—

            'DEAR FRIENDS REPENT
            NOTHING DELAY. IN MY
            YOUTH WAS I SNATCHT
                    AWAY.'

At Glympton:—

                HERE LYETH
                THE BODY OF
                HANNAH THE
            DAVGHTER OF OLIVER
            HVNT & ANNE HIS
                WIFE WHO WAS
                BVRIED DEC
                THE 4TH.
                1671.

LIKE BIRDS OF PRAY
DEATHS SNATCHT AWAY
THIS • HARMLESS DOVE
WHOSE • SOVLE • SO PVRE
IS • NOW • SECVRE
IN HEAVEN • ABOVE
1671

Time Recorders and their Makers

A sundial dated 1776, and an early Mass Dial on a quoin originally on the south, now on the west end of the south aisle about fifteen feet up, on Charlbury Church, and sundials on many of our churches, remind us of days when clocks were unknown.

One winter's morning a man working at Ditchley got up, and thinking it was time went off to work. As his mates had not arrived he climbed amongst the hay to wait, and was astonished to hear the big clock strike, I think it was, four. His mates had many a laugh at his expense.

A quaint dial stone taken out at Spelsbury was built into the wall at Coldron Mill.

Richard of Wallingford is credited with making a wonderful clock in far-away days, and after many years the craft found its stride, and in all our district clever men were engaged in it. I asked Miss Pumphrey could she tell me why many early clock-makers were Quakers. She said: 'I think I can. Quakers like doing skilful things with their hands.'

Gilks, here, when asked the price of a clock, said: 'The price is four pounds ten shillings; if thou wilt give that the clock is thine; otherwise it will remain standing in my shop.'

Thomas Wagstaff was in the first rank. Born at Banbury, married at Quakers' Meeting at Milton, died at Chipping Norton, he was on speaking terms with the king, I believe. Dan Quare was watchmaker to the Queen, and when Silvanus Bevan married his daughter Elizabeth at Friends' Meeting three hundred guests were present. Several of distinction signed the certificate, 10th November, 1715, Sarah, Duchess of Marlborough, amongst them. Jno. Nethercote's name is on various clocks. He was a wandering star, as various places are given as his residence. Wm. Green, of Milton-under-Wychwood, had a Clock Club into which so much per week was paid to get a clock.

Farbrother was a clock-maker, farmer and viol player here and at Finstock. I have heard that someone there gave him a swilling from a bucket as he was playing. Evidently he, like the rest of us, did not please everyone at all times.

Before Mr. Albright invented his phosphorus, making striking matches a practical possibility, repeating watches were made. These struck the last hour on the stem being pressed.

A bank accountant not far away had one of these, and a butcher's assistant who saw it coveted it. One night he waylaid the owner and felled him with a bludgeon, afterwards burying the watch for three days in a garden. Later he took it to a watch repairer, who found it beyond his skill and passed it to a watch-maker in the town, where it was recognised as belonging to the murdered accountant. When the deed was discovered the robber had held a lantern to light the men who carried the victim to his lodgings, and though he could not speak the dying man kept looking at him as though he wanted to say something but could not. Two men were arrested on suspicion and forty witnesses were called, but the jury threw out the bill. The guilty man confessed to the crime and was executed. The friends of the accountant saw to it that the watch-maker's son had a good start in life, and he finished his days a most genial and cordial country gentleman at Finstock. He rests in the churchyard there.

It appears a long way to-day from farriery and black-smithing to watch and clock making, but many early makers, even of the first rank, combined these crafts. Tompion, the 'father of English clock and watch making', was said to have been a farrier. A glance at an old style bedstead frame clock shows at once that to make one was a smith's job, and here, and in all the district, men fashioned these quaint old iron frame clocks. There is one by Blacksmith Mace, of Taston, at Finstock, and Viscount Dillon tells me he has one with 'Mace Ditchley' upon it, so it looks as though one of the family resided somewhere at Ditchley for a time.

The following note is of interest as showing what these country blacksmiths could do.

Bampton overseers accounts record:—

'Jan. 27, 1733. At a vestry this day held, and application being made to the said vestry by John Reynolds of Hagbourne in the County of Berks, blacksmith for payment of the sum of thirty-four pounds due to him for making a new clock and *chimes* in the parish church of Bampton, he having performed his said work according to his agreement and to the satisfaction of the vestry, therefore it is ordered by this vestry that the church wardens of this parish for the time being do forthwith pay unto the said John Reynolds the said sum of £34, according to agreement of this vestry for that purpose, except 40 shillings, which is to be left as a caution till the clock is further proved.—John Dewe, etc."

Larcum Kendall, who was Charlbury born, must have mention. He was paid £450 to reproduce faithfully the time-keeper for the Commissioners of

Longitude which Harrison had made to keep time at sea. So many lives had been lost that a very big sum was offered for such a time-keeper. Kendall made a simpler one which Captain Cook took to the Pacific and mentioned in his voyages. It also figured in the mutiny of the *Bounty*.

Matthias Padbury, a Quaker watchmaker at Burford (the son of Matthias Padbury who had a business at Sibford), married in 1774 Sh. Minchin, daughter of Anthony Minchin, of Burford butcher. This wedding took place at the Friends' Meeting House at Milton-under-Wychwood. Some who were present were Huntley, Chapoone, Fawkes and Docwra. He married again in 1785, at Burford Meeting House, Sus. Baker, daughter of Ed. Baker, of Burford, gentleman. Amongst those present were Harris, Weaver, Huntly, Luke Howard, Chris. Bowley, Chavasse, Ann and Mary Ann Lenthall (related to Speaker Lenthall, of Burford Priory?), Jermyn, Bliss, White.

Thomas Wise and his son Sam were makers here, relatives, no doubt, of the Thomas Wise who belonged to the Clock Makers' Company in 1686, who made the clock in the vestry of Westminster Abbey. Sam was quite a wag, and was very jovial. Once, as tradesmen did at hay and harvest time, he went to a farmer at Walcot and offered his services. On the farmer demurring Sam said: 'Let me go and help, *one* won't make much difference.' So he went. Later, when the farmer went to the hayfield he found Sam, as was usual, the centre of a group open of ear and mouth, but not working. He said: 'I thought you said *one* would not make much difference, but from what I can see of it, it makes *all* the difference.'

Travel by Road and Rail

In 1346 there seems to have been a toll collected for road repairs. The old British and Roman roads gave some access to the land, but travelling was difficult. A general Road Act was passed in 1555, the year of so many martyr burnings.

In 1629 a proclamation was issued that 'No common carrier or other person whatsoever should travel with any wain cart or carriage with more than two wheels, or a load of more than 20 cwts for fear of injury to the roads.' This was enforced for many years. In 1695 an Act was passed for making roads wider and setting up guide posts. Mail coaches began to run, and by 1830 travelling was a possibility.

In olden days before starting a journey you made your will, set your house in order, and hoped for the best. If a highwayman called a halt at the point of the pistol the journey did not lack spice and adventure.

The Dunsden brothers, of Fulbrook, with stores — it was said — in the forest, carried on this disgraceful business, robbing the Oxford coach of nearly £500 on one journey. They were the terror of all this district, and had their horses shod backwards so it was difficult to tell which way they had gone. Tales of robbery and murder are told about them, and the old gambling house yet standing at Capps Lodge, with cock pit in the turf near by and the gibbet tree not far away in the field, with H.D. and T.D. 1784 cut into it, show the finish of their career of crime.

There was an earlier highwayman, born at Chipping Norton, James Hinde, who carried on daring exploits of robbery and sin in high-handed fashion over a wide area. He is said to have stopped Bradshaw's coach and forced him to hand over his money, then shooting the six coach horses he rode off. He joined the Royalist Army, was betrayed and taken before Speaker Lenthall, who sent him to Newgate. Then he was sent to Reading, and later to Worcester, where he was executed, and his head was for a time on top of Worcester Bridge. Such was the mode of giving warning to all who might attempt like courses in those days.

Two highwaymen, brothers from Minster Lovell, were executed at Oxford for their crimes, I believe.

In a village on the forest border I knew an old cottage where had lived a party who possessed a cart that would travel quietly. The wheels were of wood, without iron tyres. One night it was used to fetch lead from the roof of Coggs Church, it is said.

At Oxford, in 1777, a highwayman attacked the Birmingham coach opposite the Radcliffe Infirmary and robbed a gentleman of ten guineas and a gold repeater watch. Something must be said as to the isolated position of the Infirmary in those days, as well as to the smartness of the highwayman.

Charlbury Stage Coach

Mrs. Payne writes from Fawler Mill in 1814 — 'We are accommodated with a coach to Charlbury from Ludgate Hill London. It is very convenient for this neighbourhood.'

It ran three times a week, and was called The Royal Defiance.

Vans and Waggons

Broad wheeled vans and vast tilted waggons with six to eight horses, as in Tanner and Baylis's trade card (see illustration, p. 47) were for goods and passengers. As many as 14 horses have been known to be put on one to pull it up out of the bottom near the 'Harrow' at Enstone, before the valley was raised.

Waggoner Johnson, of Charlbury, left here at 4 o'clock on Monday morning, reaching the Warwick Arms, Oxford Street, London, Wednesday mid-day; and if all went well home here on Saturday. Wards, of Chadlington, also had road waggons.

John Jolly, of Enstone, ran his waggons to Birmingham, Bromsgrove Street, daily, as well as to London; and was famous for many years. Jolly's ricks were also famous at Enstone. The men who travelled with his waggons and wonderful teams were: John Lindsay, Tom Smart, Charlie Taplin, and Charles Harris. Mr. Jolly used to wear a long smock frock, and when either of the waggons arrived home the first thing he did himself, was to grease the wheels. He rests under a big tomb at the east end of Enstone Church. An idea as to the extent of his business can be gathered from the statement that one year he lost 52 horses. They died at the rate of one per week.

I have a big horn with a chain fastened at the big end by which it used to hang on the side of a road waggon with oil or grease in it. If a wheel began to creak the waggoner could, with a big feather, anoint the big wooden axle and hub, and cracking his long whip (see picture) go smoothly on with his precious load of goods and passengers.

Very narrow by-roads are still with us, and fords are but just gone out, see Swinbrook and at Cornwell.

When vehicles met in these narrow roads one had to go back to a wider part, but much strife and anger, at times, was displayed. One story is that a man with a big waggon, and a carriage with a lady and gentleman with coachman all in style, met. It would have been easier for the carriage to back than the loaded waggon. The gentleman was instructing the coachman to do this, when the lady with great heat said, 'No, we won't hear of it.' The waggoner began to back his team, saying to the gentleman, 'All right, sir, I've got just such another one at home.'

John Woolman

'On the 8th of sixth month 1772 we landed at London,' so writes John Woolman, and he tramped through Hertford, Warwick, Oxford, and Nottingham to York. He records, 'First of 7th mo.—I have been at Quarterly Meetings at Banbury and Shipton, and have had sundry meetings between.' Again on the 17th he records Warwick and Oxfordshire.

Charles Lamb said, 'Get the writings of John Woolman by heart.' Others know the rare sweetness and purity of the record of his life. What has he to say re conditions as he found them hereabouts?

'On inquiry in many places I find the price of rye about five shillings; wheat, 8s. per bushel; oatmeal, 12s. for 120 lbs.; mutton, 3d. to 5d.; bacon, 7d. to 9d.; cheese, 4d. to 6d; butter, 8d. to 10d.; house rent for a poor man, 25s. to 40s. per year paid weekly; wood for fire scarce and dear; coal in some places 2s. 6d. per cwt.; near the pits not a quarter as much. O may the wealthy consider the poor.

'The wages of labouring men near London 10d. per day, with small beer found. Harvest and hay time about 1s. per day, and food and drink. Women in factories got from 4d. to 10d. per day. Many live on bread and water chiefly, and many children are not taught to read. May those who have abundance lay these things to heart.'

FLY WAGGONS.

EVERY MORNING & EVENING *(Sunday Excepted)* IN TWO DAYS
each way conveying Goods to, and from, the
GLOUCESTERSHIRE WAREHOUSE 33 WHITE CROSS STREET CRIPPLEGATE

London,

their Warehouses. Winchcomb Street, Cheltenham
AND WESTGATE STREET, GLOUCESTER,
and all parts of the Counties of Gloucester, Hereford. Monmouth
and South Wales,

Bath Bristol, the West, Ireland, &c?

WAGGONS DAILY.

TO & FROM THE BELL INN THOMAS STREET, BRISTOL,
AND N: 20 CORN STREET, BATH.

Conveyances from all parts of the West meet at Bristol,
where, Goods are also Shipped. for Ireland, &c.
Luggage or Goods consigned to Tanner & Baylis
promptly forwarded to any place in England Wales or Scotland.

NB *Not accountable for Package or Parcel above the value of*
Five Pounds unless entered as such & paid for accordingly.

TANNER & BAYLIS'S

Regular & Expeditious Fly Vans,

PECULIARLY
ADAPTED
FOR
LUGGAGE &c

TO AND FROM
LONDON,
IN 20 HOURS
EACH WAY.

TO & FROM THE
GLOUCESTERSHIRE WAREHOUSE 33 WHITE CROSS ST? CRIPPLEGATE,
LONDON

Every Tuesday, Thursday & Saturday at Noon. arriving at their.
Warehouse. Winchcomb Street. CHELTENHAM in Twenty Hours.& at their
. Warehouse. Westgate Street Gloucester. in Twenty Two hours.

Baylis's Trade Card showing Road Waggon and Fly Van

He would not use the stage coach for his journeys, and was not free to send letters by them, because horses were driven to death or blindness, and the poor post boys rode under terrible conditions, some were even frozen to death. 'So great is the hurry in the spirit of this world, that in aiming to do business quickly and to gain wealth, the creation at this day doth loudly groan.'

CHARLBURY CARRIER

One night when the Charlbury carrier was returning from Witney, after leaving Finstock, to balance his load (he had some timbers and no passenger) he got up on the back end and rode, letting Jerry, the horse, have his head. When they were down in the low part near the river, (where the road then was can be seen from the embankment) he heard a voice call out, and the horse stopped. Jumping down, he ran round to see if it was friend or foe, and it was evidently not the former, for whoever it was had up and through the hedge, and entirely disappeared. The carrier was known to carry pistols, andl everyone knew he was not a man to trifle with.

Bakers took bread about on donkeys' backs in basket panniers. Mr. G. J. Jones told me of one of his kin who used to carry the money he had taken for bread in his boots, in case he should be compelled to turn out his pockets, as many did, to some gentleman of the road who might turn up anywhere.

CHADLINGTON

In winter time, when the mail could not be got from Oxford because of frost and snow, Thomas Townsend would walk to Oxford from Chadlington by 8 o'clock in the morning; going out in fields, over hedges, and ditches, because of the snow, carrying the mail.

Once the race horse, Coronation, went for them. His keeper, Paintin, rode him the 19 miles to Oxford in half an hour, it is said. Coronation could move, he won the Derby in 1841, beating 28 others. He was bred by Mr. Abraham Rawlinson at Chadlington, and when he won the Derby Chipping Norton church bells were rung to celebrate the event.

THE RAILWAY

The coming of the railway was a most eventful thing for these parts. Out of the way, as we had been, somewhat off the main road, and then to find ourselves in touch with the great metropolis and all between, and away to the west, wonders on wonders.

Tidings reached us about this wonder, and some refused to believe. A friend tells me how a post boy, who went from Enstone with his horse to Birmingham, and came home and told of the wonder, 'a train, an engine', was not believed. His father said, 'Wait till our so and so comes home, we shall know the rights about it.' Meantime the boy was not believed.

When the railway reached Oxford my father walked there one day to see a train, and then came back without the sight. He told me he had said, when it was talked about being extended here, that it would never pay to bring a railway to these parts.

BRADSHAW'S GUIDE

This was first published in 1839, 19th 10 Mo., price 6d. The second (so-called) is before me, dated 10th Mo. 25th, 1839, and as it has printed No. 3 either that is a mistake or there was another between this and the first. It is a tiny book and was priced at one shilling. It has some beautiful little maps. It was issued, indeed, by a Quaker engraver to sell his maps, and it met a need at the same time. The issue (1st. Mo. 1840) I have in my hand is also No. 3, according to the figure printed inside the cover. Evidently there is some mistake somewhere. The size is about four and a half by three inches, and a quarter of an inch thick, with strong covers. The earliest copy I have shows services from London to Birmingham, London to Twyford, Birmingham to Liverpool and Manchester. It is stated:—

> First class trains consist of First Class and Mail carriages, carrying four inside (one compartment of which is convertible into a bed carriage, if required). The Mixed trains consist of First Class carriages carrying six inside and of Second Class carriages closed and entirely protected from the weather. Each carriage has a small roof lamp by day and night.
> No smoking is allowed at the stations or in the company's carriages.
> All the company's servants are strictly enjoined on pain of dismissal, to observe the utmost civility and attention towards all passengers.
> Passengers are especially recommended to have their names and address, or destination, legibly written on each part of their luggage, when it will be placed on the top of the coach in which they ride, unless it be in a bag or such other small package as may conveniently be taken under the seats inside, opposite the one they occupy.

A RAIL MAN'S STORY

A group of railwaymen 'packers' were on the line not far from here some years ago when a Blenheim shooting party came into the fields near, and the then Duke of Marlborough came and chatted to them. The express was heard to be coming and all stood clear, but the Duke was seen to place a florin on the rail. When the train had swept past all were looking for the coin, but it was nowhere to be found. As soon as his Grace had gone one of the men moved his foot, disclosing the coin, which he had kept thus hidden.

'The Concord of Sweet Sounds'

The love children have for 'the concord of sweet sounds' found gratification at Finstock in various ways. The songs of birds, and nature's chorus we could hear all about us, the ploughboy's whistle, and the sweet voice of a woman singing at her work when her heart was glad. And occasionally some travelling musician would come along.

Whistling Charley, when he came our way, was a wonder to be listened to and talked about. Once a Scotch bag piper came. This was an event of the first order, and to see and hear him excited all the interest which attaches to a new experience.

There is a story of a noble lord who wished to engage a piper for some occasion. He applied to Queen Victoria's piper as to where he could get one, and describing what was wanted said: 'Just such another piper as youreslf.' He received an answer something like this: 'Lords such as yourself in plenty, but very few sic pipers as me.'

Ours was fine, never to be forgotten.

Sometimes we heard a fiddle. That was very delightful to our young ears, but generally the associations with drink, dancing, shame and sorrow made it not quite the thing for some I know. I sat by the bedside of a fiddler and I remember he said to me: 'I have gone with my fiddle to Field Town Club for the two days, and I have brought home more money than both the bands had, but the money was no good.' As he lay ill, looking at life as it was, this was his summing up. An old book I have gives a verdict somewhat similar in the words, 'Vanity ... all is vanity.'

Pleasant memories linger about the music George Dring used to get from a squarish shaped concertina which as a lad he used to play, standing under his mother's mountain ash tree nearly opposite to Finstock School. It was far more agreeable than *some* of the wireless so-called music, which is 'Knock, knock, knock; bang, bang, bang,' etc. Those with no knowledge of the science of music delight to hear it, and like the boy who said, 'He could not do the cooking, but he knew when they had a good dinner,' harmonious music is much enjoyed.

MUSIC IN WORSHIP

When Methodism arose congregational singing was almost unknown. There were but few hymns to sing, with tunes of few varieties. It is recorded in 1762 that the tune 'York' was sung fifteen times in one week at one church. Wesley's hymns gave greater variety. Watts had done much with his hymns. It should be remembered that both Baptists and Quakers held even Psalm singing a carnal ordinance, and for a time the Baptist body was split into singing and non-sing congregations. In our neighbourhood Benjamin Beddome, M.A., the splendid

Baptist minister at Bourton-on-Water, used to prepare a hymn weekly, to be sung after Sunday morning sermon.

Charles Frederick Lampe was Wesley's first tune writer. He played the bassoon in Handel's band and wrote music for Covent Garden Theatre, of which he became lessee, but he got converted through reading Wesley's tract, *An Appeal to Men of Reason.* This occasioned Chas. Wesley to write his 'Musician's Hymn.' It is in a small hymn book I have, published by Wesley in 1761 and containing 51 hymns. I will give a verse:—

'With *Tubal's* wretched sons no more
I prostitute my sacred Power
To please the Fiends beneath,
Or modulate the wanton Lay,
Or smooth with Musick's hand the way
To everlasting Death.'

Handel, at the request of Mrs. Rich, wife of Rich the comedian, who became a serious person under Methodist influence, wrote tunes for Wesley. Though Handel was a very profane man, and would swear in three languages when provoked, they all met at Lampe's house. (Handel was a different man when old and blind.)

Scores of old song tunes got pressed into service — 'Sweet Anne Page', 'Few Happy Matches', and the tune called 'Prospect' was that to Ben Jonson's 'Drink to me, etc.' It is in use to-day.

Instruments followed in the wake of the pitch pipe. This was a wooden whistle about a foot in length, with a piston inside. The piston had the notes marked on one side and was withdrawn to get the right note. Some were offended at this innovation. A minute of the Methodist Conference of 1805 reads: 'Let no instrument of music be introduced into the singers' seat except a bass viol.' In spite of this there was soon a regular band in chapel and church.

My grandfather took the bass viol in Charlbury Church once, I heard, when the regular performer could not be there. At other times he played the flute.

In church the fiddle was opposed and had to be played wrong end up. This separated it from the tavern and secular fiddling and made it a viol. The bass viol player when it was warm would take off his coat, this sometimes giving offence. The tuning during the giving out of the hymn or Psalm was not liked, and it was said, ' Now we have only catgut and raz-zum (rosin) worship.'

Flutes and a concertina were used in Finstock Chapel before the harmonium came along.

One of Wesley's preachers wrote him: 'Long ago I desired Bro. W. Kersey to forbear singing between prayer and text... Last Sat. I told him in your name, "Mr. Wesley desires you would sing no more than twice."'

Wesley wrote these men:—

London,
Dec. 14, 1784.

If you do not choose to obey me you need not, I will send other preachers in your place. If you choose to stay with me, never sing more than twice, once before and once after sermon.

Your affectionate brother,

J. WESLEY.

After the bands, barrel organs came in. The 'Grinstun organ', as it was called, had so many tunes on a barrel. Some of these tunes were not always hymn tunes, as at Coggs Church. Theirs was not all sacred music, and I have heard that if a lad could, unobserved slip along the index finger and get one of these secular, if not profane, tunes started, he thought he had done a clever thing.

The Oxford Movement brought in pipe organs, harmoniums, choirs with surplices, the latter for the lads to wear. This, I know, drove some from church, never to enter till they were carried there. They looked uniform, and it was thought seemly. One thinks of the tale told of the old lady who said: 'They looks like angels, but I knows 'em.' Not all like these boys by a long way, are they ?

SONGS

We heard snatches of 'A starry night for a ramble, amid the flowery dell', 'Up in a baloon, boys', 'Jump into the waggon', 'Pull for the shore', 'Never miss the water till the well runs dry', 'Tommy make room for your uncle', 'Over the garden wall', 'Grandfather's Clock', etc., but there were many who never dreamt of using these songs, though they could not be unaware of their use. I know the plane of religious life on which they lived was beyond. 'Take my voice and let me sing, always only for my King,' as Miss Havergal's hymn so finely puts it, was their rule, and humble cottage folk walked in the high places of religious life and experience, and the greater, naturally, excludes the less. Did not George Fox say 'I am on top of the world'?

I am glad as a lad we sang and heard sung hymns about heaven: 'There is a happy land', 'What must it be to be there?' and others. The difficult times the working people had no doubt helped to make such hymns popular, apart from their spiritual aspect. Very many have felt comfort and hope, when in times of trouble and heartbreak and death the mind has swung back, as it does, to the fundamental things learnt in one's earliest days. I am afraid the present generation have not this treasure which does not 'wax old'.

Wychwood

See! dawn breaks, painting leaf and tree,
   Old Wychwood dons its robe of green,
Now, at our feet, what joy to see,
   Its rolling sweep of glorious sheen.

Fair scenes; here beast and bird
   Find safe retreat 'gainst man's alarm,
Rare blossoms too; by lake and sward,
   Come to perfection, safe from harm.

Thy billowy shape; when autumn's hue,
   By angel hands has been o'er spread,
(Its setting is the arc of blue),
   Joy!, Wychwood lives, it is not dead.

Gay hearted youth and life in bloom,
   Has lightly danced thy ways along.
Speak softly; tread lightly; some full soon
   Found darksome deed; a dirge; not song.

Yet dark or light, man's deeds apart,
   Kind nature sings its wondrous psalm,
And blest are they with cleansed heart,
   That know the great Creator's balm.

Forest Places

Ascott-under-Wychwood

Estcott

The name means, evidently, 'the east home or cottage', and if, as possibly long ago was the case, it was a connection of Shipton, away to the west, the name simply fell to it. When travel led men to know there were other East Cotes, or cots, the Forest easily lent its famous name and all was clear — Ascott-under-Wychwood.

The church, dedicated to the Holy Trinity, groups well and makes a model picture of an Oxfordshire village church. The Norman entrance to the quaint porch and the nave-arcade at once give a clue as to the early date, when reverent men built more strongly for what they felt was God's honour than for any other building in the parish. There are Perpendicular features, the font and the tower and windows, and there are original oak seats. Many churches had no such luxuries, straw and rushes being strewn on the floor, upon which the worshippers stood or knelt. So Ascott was quite to the fore, with seats in the church.

Coins turn up about the village. I possess a small one which I think, from the device upon it, is a British coin. A broken rapier was brought to me in the churchyard there one day by a worthy man, who said, 'I was just going to use this, with some Iron bars, to help set a copper, and I thought you might like it.' He thought aright. It had an inscribed Spanish blade and an English hilt. I wondered what its history might be — if it was broken in some affray in the forest near by and left, after the encounter, to be picked up by some villager and stored for many, many years in a cottage attic, seeing daylight when the copper setter asked, 'had they any iron bars he could use?' And then his kind thought of me.

There is a stone coffin just discernible in the turf at the north side of the church, possibly brought out of the building at some time. Many finely cut gravestones were at some time taken up and now stand against a wall. They ought to be set in the ground somewhere, even if the old grave sites are lost.

There is a big tump or mound in a garden nearly opposite the Tiddy Hall. Is it a barrow?

When I was a lad I saw human remains near the surface at the Quarry at the London Turn on the Charlbury road. Tools were to be found at a quarry, and when a dark deed meant secret burial it was to the quarry that guilty men hurried, and up on the bank near-by hastily buried their dead.

THE BAPTIST CHAPEL

This modest little chapel, originally a malthouse, was opened in 1816. For many years Mr. Thomas Parsons, of Chipping Norton, conducted a Sunday school at Cleveley in the morning, at Ascott in the afternoon, and preached at night. Students from Mr. Grey's school who assisted him were nicknamed 'greyhounds'. He lived to be 94. Though in early days the chapel had to be closed for a time, the work has been carried on through evil and good report, through persecution, but yet much blessing, and the services and school continue.

THE MANOR HOUSE

I heard a story long ago about someone who went away from this house leaving upon the table an open Bible with the words marked: 'The master of the house has gone a long journey. He has taken a bag of money with him.'

I do not think he was heard of again.

Asthall

ASTHALL. ESTHVILL, 1245

The village lies low down in the Windrush valley, so that formerly the water at flood times would rise to the level of the cottage windows and, I heard a native say, would go into his waistcoat pockets. The Church and Manor House are on rising ground out of the flood area.

The church, with its big chancel, north transept with female effigy, beneath carved work, is worth seeing. A very unusual stone altar with piscina attached is here. The arches and stonework are Late Norman to Early English. The roof corbels are modern. There is a small Perpendicular West Tower, and high up on the south wall is a small niche where was a figure long ago.

The Manor House looks heavy, broad and lumpy, giving the impression that there would be room to move about inside.

In the village, if I remember aright, a panel in a barn bears the name of Fletcher, and when I stayed at the place as a lad, I used to have in my mind that he was one of the persecuted men of the place who had the Word of God and suffered for it in days of yore.

One day smoke came pouring out of an old farm house occupied by a labourer whose wife had gone out, leaving the children in charge. Part of the house was used as a store for wool. The smoke was choking, and it was a puzzle to locate the fire. I crept on hands and knees round one room in search of it, and then a man who was working with us found that some woollen garments left before a fire were burning. In a day or two word came to us that there was a pint of beer each awaiting us at the public house for our work at the fire. As neither father nor I took it, the delight of the man who was working with us at the thought that he would have the three pints, I shall never forget.

Akeman Street is near-by, and recently some of it was laid bare. Also work has been done at the remarkable barrow away on the hill. Along in the valley is the site of what was possibly a Roman villa.

There was a story of a ghost, 'Old Blue Stockings', to be seen in the meadow, but I did not have the pleasure of making his acquaintance when I was about that way. Another story was told of a phantom team on the main road. I remember that a farmer who used to come and talk to rny father, said one day: 'When we were in bed my wife said, "Philip, there is someone in the house; I can hear them," but I said to her, "Put your head under the clothes and let us die like men."'

The arrow head (Fig. III) was found in the meadows towards Swinbrook.

Burford

My first sight of this gem of a forest town was one summer's evening with my father, long ago. We saw Shipton Barrow, then he took me over the Downs far enough to see Burford, and the sight and pleasurable anticipation of some day visiting it, remain as a fragrant memory. Later on I was able to walk its streets, where there is much to notice — cunning work in stone, and wood, and iron, and slate; walls, windows, roofs, verges, railings. The Tolsey, the Great House, the Priory, the bridge, the almshouses, the schools, the chapels, the church, and all between, make a most interesting and delightful assemblage, with fact, story and legend of great charm.

Much has been noticed, sought out and lovingly recorded in pages penned by Fisher, Gretton, Monk, Paintin — to give a few outstanding names who have earned the gratitude of a host of readers far and wide.

Burford being on a road, and a Windrush crossing, and close to the Royal Forest of Wychwood, was, by reason of these factors, of importance in many ways.

It was a place of call and refreshment, as well as a market. Merchants, pedlars, mountebanks and pilgrims, all found it a desirable place to visit.

The story of Burford goes back to the days of the battle of A.D. 752. The quaint bridge, with its recesses for foot passengers to step into, could tell a story, and the bridge tolls of 1322 give to us some idea of the importance of the trade of the town in those far-off days. Many kings and royalties visited it; some ate and drank and slept there. War, stern, cruel, wicked war, touched it. At Bosworth and other famous fields its sons played their parts, and the clash of arms has not been unknown in the streets of Burford itself. The western wall of the churchyard has bullet marks which show where executions took place in some of the stern and difficult days of the past.

Many able pens have described the splendid church. Its length, its wondrous chapels, its monuments, the 'prisner's' name in the lead in the font. The altars were swept away before Cromwell was born. His men, and possibly Royalist troops, were quartered in the church. The figures in the porch niches possibly had their heads shot off, or punched off with a pole, by Edward VI's Commissioners. A pity? Yes, but after such things as had taken place, something gets bumped or punched, and not always a head of stone. So we may be sorry, and not judge too severely.

We think, too, of those who suffered for love of God's Word and for trying to do as they thought it directed them. We would do well to remember Archbishop Chicheley's mandate that three persons in every parish should be examined thrice every year, upon oath, and required to inform against any persons they knew who differed in life or manners from catholic men, or who had any suspected books. Such non-conformists had to do penance, stand on the cross steps, or carry a faggot. Remembering all this, we are devoutly thankful that wiser counsels prevail.

Great names figure in Burford story — Warwick the 'King Maker', Tanfield, Cary, Lenthall, and others.

Wesley preached to vast congregations at Burford, being entertained at Mr. Maizey's house.

John Hancock, whose signature figures so boldly on the Declaration of the Independence of America, is said to have been of Quaker descent, from Burford or near-by.

CROMWELL'S MEN IN CHURCHES

Cromwell's and Royalist men sleeping on straw within the churches, waiting the dawn and stress of another day, must be thought of in the light of other days than these. We must remember many things were done formerly in churches unthinkable to-day. The bell-founder would dig his pits, erect his furnace and with his bellows fill all the place with smoke; and more strange than this, the Morris dancers would first dance in the church before starting on their round of the parish. St. Helen's churchwardens' accounts at Abingdon record 'two dozen merres belles were bought by the parish for 1/-.' Wool was stored, and on occasion treasure chests put there, wakes and fairs were held within and stalls set up for the sale of victuals.

An old will records that: 'The next Sunday after her burial there be 24 loaves, a kilderkin of ale, two gammons of bacon, three shoulders of mutton, two couples of rabbits, desiring all the parish, as well rich as poor, to take part thereof, and a table be set in the midst of the church with everything necessary thereto.' Of course cock-fighting and card playing could not be but occasional evil uses — not a custom, only wanton impiety. But to sleep the night there for shelter would not be thought anything out of place, or even its use as a prison.

Charlbury's fire engine was from its earliest days until quite recent years housed in the church.

The village armour was often kept in the church till in those stern days it was wanted. A turkey and possibly other fowls have been put to sit on eggs in the church in the days when services were few and far between.

Bladon

The village bears the former name of the river Evenlode.

Doomsday records a pottery yielding 10/-. (Bladon bricks, known by their small size, are in buildings about the district.) There are recorded two slaves, two villeins, and 18 cottars and a wood three miles long.

In 1279 some tenants paid 3/9 a year, also doing work for the lord. When reaping each man was to have a sheaf as big as he could carry to his door with his hook, and when carrying at Leggen-acre as much hay as he could raise with his rake.

In 1300 the King's birds and hawks were in charge of Bladon men, whilst one carried a banner, for which he had certain land and 2d. a day from the King's purse.

In 1262 Bladon was given to Eynsham Abbey.

The church is modern. A tiny stone coffin lid, with ornament carved in relief, is preserved there — perhaps the only visible remnant of the ancient parish church of the Royal borough of Woodstock, where, no doubt, many of our kings had worshipped when in residence there.

The living was given at the Restoration to the Rev. Matthew Griffiths, who had fought in the war. A sermon of his called forth a reply from John Milton, and his devotion to the Liturgy had caused those in power to give him the sight of the inside of a prison more than once. He died at Bladon in peaceful days, as he was preaching in 1665.

'Round Castle', on the Heath, is an early earthwork, the origin of which is lost in obscurity.

I want to put on record a most worthy bit of recent village life. A few years ago, when I was staying there, a man was badly hurt in a road accident and lay at the Radcliffe Infirmary insensible for many days. During this time when his life was in the balance (it was in the spring) some thirty of the men of the place assembled one evening on his allotment with their garden tools and very quickly put it in order, doing all that was necessary. I feel sure the angels must have smiled that night, and it always does me good to think of it.

THE CHAPELS

There are two chapels — the Primitive Methodist and the Wesleyan.

A worthy man, lovingly referred to as Daddy Summers to this day, settled in the place in 1818, and opened his house on Sunday evening for reading the Scriptures and the singing of a few hymns. There was only one service a week at the parish church. This cottage gathering continued for many years. John Summers used to walk to Freeland Wesleyan Chapel for the six o'clock Sunday morning prayer meeting, carrying the baby, whilst his wife carried the lantern. John Collins had the Methodist class meeting, led by Mr. Summers, at his house. That meeting continues to this day, having only had three leaders in about a century.

The first chapel was built in 1843; the present one in 1877. The jubilee celebrations were held on June 19th, 1927. A glorious past; a noble heritage.

Long Combe, or Coombe

This village, clustered around its green with an ancient tree upon it, provides us with much that is of interest. A piece of ring money found here is on show at the Ashmolean Museum, and I have heard that others were picked up by a person who, walking by the river, thoughtlessly threw them, one by one, into the water, as if they were small pebbles.

Doomsday: Cumbe, 1 hide. Originally Cwm or Cum, Welsh to-day for valley. Odo lord of the manor, 120 acres arable, 15 of meadow.

In 1141 the Empress Matilda gave the church to Eynsham Abbey. In 1279 the mill was worth 3/-.

Early in its history the village was moved from the valley to the hill top, the church being taken up to its present site in 1395. The north, or 'Devil's door', has a porch roofed with stone which is worth notice. The stone pulpit against the north wall is also an object of interest. There are roof timbers, old glass, and an ancient stone which was used for years as a well head. This latter is thought by some to have been the font. The wall paintings were uncovered in 1894, and ought to be seen. A most unfortunate fire in the belfry destroyed some things of interest. It was sad to see the broken bells where they fell. The old chest and documents, the original Perpendicular west doors, and the clarinet, mounted on a board, which the late Mr. Stoker used to play in the church, all perished.

A gold ring with a big ruby in it was found in the churchyard some years ago.

In 1478 the church and rectory went into the care of Lincoln College, Oxford, and the statutes state that twice a year the Rector shall supervise the Rectory, three and sixpence to be allowed for his expenses; and during two weeks in Lent one of the college Fellows shall assist the chaplain there. The college accounts show that in 1731 John Wesley was sent to discharge this duty.

The Bodleian records show that the church has been the place of public penance more than once. These unseemly and painful spectacles are, fortunately, gone for ever.

'1549. John White, of Combe, and Richard Tompson, of Dunstew, to be hanged at Banbury.'

On Whit Sunday, June 9th, 1549, the new Prayer Book was to be used in the churches. Legendary and some other matter, 'uncertain stories, legendes, responds, verses, vaine repetitions, commemoraciens, and synodulles' were, it was thought, better away.

The new book was

Imprinted at London in
Fletestrete, at the sign of the Sunne ouer against
the conduyt by EdVVarde VVhitchurche.
The seuenth daye of Marche, the
yeare of our Lorde,
1549.
The Kinges Maiestie
the aduyse of his most deare uncle the Lord Pro-
tector and other his highnes Counsell, streightly
chargeth and commaundeth, that no maner
of person do sell this present booke un-
bounde, aboue the price of ii. Shyllynges the piece. And the
same bounde in paste or
in boordes, not aboue
the price of three
shyllynges and
fourepence
the piece.
GOD SAUE THE KYNG.

Spelling and type-setting are somewhat original, as will be seen from the title page given above.

Much opposition was given to the book by those who loved the Mass and resented images and roods being removed from the churches. Berkshire and Oxfordshire were very decidedly against it, and there were riots. Lord Grey de Wilton was sent to quell these, and after consultation with the upper ten at Witney, examples were made by hanging a few clergy, the Vicar of Combe being one, as a warning to the countryside.

THE CHAPELS

Combe has a Wesleyan chapel, and at the time of the disruption a Wesleyan Reform chapel was built, and the two have both done very well and helped to foster the religious life of the place. Those who know the village consider that the two have been none too many. Unity is possible without union.

One is reminded of the story of a parish clerk who used to attend the evening service at the village chapel. One day his vicar told him he thought he would conduct an evening service at the church. The clerk, taken by surprise, said: 'Then I shall not be able to get to a place of worship at all, sir.'

Enstone

ENNESTAN, 1350. ENSTAN, 1400.

Any account of this remarkable and interesting parish must certainly mention 'The Parochial History of Enstone' (1856), by the Rev. J. Jordan. I well remember as a lad being lent a copy by good, kind Mrs. Alderton. When later as a youth I used to tramp in frosty weather and visit the churches in our district, it was with curious satisfaction I feasted my eyes upon the church he so well describes. Within were books with chains to them which arrested me. 'Foxe's Martyrs' (1590), etc. I have for years missed them and wondered sadly where they had gone, but recently Mr. Hawtin, the clerk, told me they were locked up in the safe. That is well, so far, but if they were displayed in a good glass case within the church the joy of seeing them could be shared by all, while they, or their chains, could not be touched by curious, careless or profane hands.

THE HOAR STONE

The name Enstone is said to be derived from two Saxon words, 'Enta', 'Stan', the giant's stone. The Hoar Stone, as it is called, is at the cross roads where the Charlbury to Banbury road is crossed by the Enstone to Fulwell roads. Thousands have passed, and still pass, without the slightest idea of what is

The Hoar Stone as it used to be

buried amongst the holly bushes just over the wall. This cromlech has fallen. It was formerly supported on three stones, two of which are broken. It looked like a big sentry box, with the opening due east. The dimensions will give some idea as to its importance. They are as follows: Principal upright standing, height about 10ft., width, 6ft. 10in., thickness 3ft. 6in.; table stone, length 9ft., width 8ft., thickness, 3ft. to 2ft.

THE CHURCH

The Church of St. Edward the Confessor (it was originally of St. Kenelm) is entered by a beautiful late Norman doorway, over which a porch with chamber above has been erected. Early English and late Norman work appears within the church. There were originally twelve pillars, some of which were circular and some octagonal with each face a flat hollow. They were evidently late in period. There were five arches on each side, but when the tower was built at the west end the arches were interfered with. The chancel, clerestory and porch possibly were all erected about the same time. The embattled tower is stumpy. There used to be a rood screen and loft, but this was removed not so many years ago. There were stone seats against some of the walls, so that cripples and weakly worshippers could sit, others stood or knelt on straw. The field name, 'Litter Acre' is evidence of this. One of these seats was found to have underneath it a stone coffin of about 1440. A wide Tudor arch opens from a south chapel which has in the eastern wall a small stone altar, the three light window above it with niches forming a reredos, the three lights signifying the Divine number, the Trinity. The ancient glass should be noticed here.

Five altars are thought to have been in this church in pre-Reformation days. No doubt the thought behind this number was the five wounds of Our Lord. A finely sculptured marble tablet is on the north wall to the memory of Mr. Benjamin Marten, who left £120, the interest to be laid out in meat for twenty poor parishioners of Enstone and Radford (1715). In the chancel floor are ponderous well-carved slabs, 'Cole', 'Walker', 'Stonehouse', with arms, etc., upon them. Stevens Wisdom, XXIII Apreel, 1633, left £10 to the poor for ever, and has a remarkable effigy and memorial in the south chapel.

A gallery used to be in the west end of the nave, and a band of various instruments led the singing. One thinks of the story of those days when, a very long psalm being announced at a church, one performer said to the bass viol player: 'Now Bill, off with thy jacket; we be in for a lathering now.'

THE CHURCH BELLS

The bells were re-cast in 1831, and fortunately the inscriptions on the old bells have been preserved:—

4th: 'Matthew Bayle made me 1767. Thos. Kinch, Henry Lay, churchwardens.'

5th: 'Richard Keene (Woodstock founder) made this ring 1661.'

6th: 'Matthew Bayle made me 1769.

'I to the church the living call,

And to the grave I summon all.'

The church accounts for 1787 record: 'Pd. for new casting the sance bell, £1 11s. 11½d.' This bell has gone.

KING CHARLES I AND HIS MINT MASTER, THOMAS BUSHELL, OF ENSTONE

In December, 1642, the King issued a proclamation for establishing a mint at Oxford, and Thomas Bushell, Esquire, of Enstone, took charge, with his men, hammers and dies. In the previous year King Charles had had large sums of money from the Oxford colleges. Now he issues letters to them that their plate is to be brought to the mint, 'there to be coyned into money'. The colleges offered to pay money to save their precious plate from our Enstone man's dies, but finally it had to be surrendered. St. John's paid £800 and saved theirs for a time, but a very nice letter went from Charles to the college, and over two hundred pounds weight of plate went to 'Thos. Bushell, Esq., Officer of our Mint'. The money made from this plate had the letter B stamped on it because the president's name was Richard Baylie. One of these coins, a shilling, is before me. It bears on the margin 'Exvrgat: Devs: Dissipentvr: Inimici:' (Let God arise; let His enemies be scattered).

Bushell was a Balliol College man, and a gift he made to the Queen got him in favour, and being a man of parts he was appointed 'farmer of the King's minerals in Wales'. This paid him well, and he 'did cloath the King's army at Oxford.'

The famous water works, cascades, nightingale's song, etc., he made at Enstone have entirely gone. The King and Queen were at the opening ceremony, and it is told how as many as sixteen coaches with four horses to each have been seen waiting at one time for those who had come to take part in gaieties there. The banqueting house did its last service as a carpenter's shop.

Soon Mr. Bushell had to go into hiding, and but for the faithfulness of an old woman and his manservant he would have lost his life. Someone interceded with Cromwell for him after a time, and he lived to be eighty years of age. A man of genius, able to show the way, but he did not himself arrive.

THE COACHES, ETC.

One bitter winter's night, when the stage coach arrived at Enstone, the driver was found to be dead. He had perished in the cold after leaving Chapel House.

The inns were busy places in the coaching days. I will give a little jingle I heard about their names:

'The "Harrow" to harrow,
The "Plough" to plow,
The "Swan" to swim,
The "Bell" to ring,
The "Litchfield Arms",
And the "Talbot" Inn.'

The 'Talbot' was so named in honour of Earl Shrewsbury, of Heythrop, a Roman Catholic, who used to entertain all who went to the chapel in the park, till the numbers got so great that he said ' from what he could see they were not all Roman Catholics, but Roman platter licks.'

'LUDSTON' WATER MILL

A fine old parchment deed in a bold hand exists which shows that 'ffairmeadow Penyston of Cornwell and Edmund Gooyear of Heythrop, leased for one year to Joseph Harris miller all that water mill at Ludston in the parish of Enstone for the sum of six shillings good and lawful money of England.' (1700). Through many vicissitudes, as indicated in a number of vast parchments, the mill got into the hands of Thomas Day Savery, who was evidently interested in Methodism, as indicated by his last will and testament.

METHODISM

Thomas Savery, of Lidston Mill, left £20 to Richard Wheeler, Samuel West and James Taylor in trust to be applied for and towards erecting a Methodist chapel now about to be built at Neat Enstone, 1811. The men who carried this work through at that time were Richard Cooke, of Chipping Norton, Thomas Herbert, Enstone, Wm. H. Attwood, of Cherrington, Thos. Bennett, Edward Bennett, Wm. Jones, Wm. Collins, Robert Hunt, John Turner, Thos. Jarvis, Wm. Jacques, Jeremiah Biggers, of Witney, and Henry Leake.

'The same preacher shall not be sent to the said chapel for more than two years successively without the consent of the trustees in writing.' This is in the constitution of the place. A gallery was put in, and about 1870 the schoolroom was built. The stalwarts were Edward Bennett, Robert Jones, William Kibble, Edward Paxford, Thomas Savage, Thos. Hitchcox, Thomas Bennett. The latter was a born preacher of extraordinary eloquence and power. On many occasions he walked to Stow-on-the-Wold for morning service, then to Westcote in the afternoon, and back to Stow for evening, preaching three times, then walking home — altogether over forty miles.

SCHOOLS

The National Schools, built in 1836, had as master Mr. William Kibble, who at first used to walk over from Charlbury. He told me some of the lads used to meet him on Banbury Hill in the morning. He was for fifty years post-master (Enstone was head office for this district), a local preacher for the whole of the period, a churchwarden, and he also held other parish offices. He seems to have pretty well filled his day.

Mr. John Adams was schoolmaster for many years and later postmaster. Charlbury letters used to be fetched from Enstone in a cart drawn by a dog. It was certain the mail was never late through engine trouble or puncture in those days!

At Enstone were dwelling at one time, it is said, persons named Pope, Bishop, Parson, Clark, Sexton and Sirman.

Cleveley, Radford and Lidstone

In Cleveley an early doorway in what is now a cottage must have mention. A poor demented person some years ago was fastened with a chain to the floor here. A Baptist chapel and cause are in the hamlet.

At Lidston is a Primitive Methodist chapel. A camp meeting used to be held at Chalford Green.

The Roman Catholic church and schools at Radford remind us that the faith as taught in that communion is amongst us.

Fulbrook

A pretty little cluster of houses with an interesting church with small western tower and south doorway, partly Norman. To the right of this, behind an altar tomb, at the foot of the south wall can be seen some early walling, stones set edge-wise. The mason 'Seacole' tablet is within the church, with 'Castle' upon it, similar to the 'mason's' mark cut on the right hand quoin of what is now the Wesleyan chapel at Burford, the same sign appearing on the end of a big tomb at the left of the path leading to Taynton Church door, to the memory of one Newman, a mason of that place.

There used to be many workers in metal at Fulbrook. I have heard it referred to as 'Tinker Town.' I stayed a few nights some years ago at the old house said to have been the home of the notorious Dunsdens, two of whom were gibbeted at Capps Lodge not far away.

I obtained at this place a store of parts of old flint locks to which poachers used to go for fittings, springs, etc., to repair their guns.

Glympton

Glympton, with its stocks, is so shut off from the world by its position and its many trees, that its quiet is a hushed enchantment, and one feels that the old settlers knew how to select a spot for a dwelling and a church. They loved the snug peace of a sheltered valley and trees about them, a brook for water and in which to fish, the song of birds all round them, meadows aglow with buttercups in spring, and violets and primroses in their turn, about their feet.

Doomsday records the Bishop of Constance as owner.

THE CHURCH

The Church of St. Mary, much restored, has features of interest — the chancel arch, the tower, the Tesdale brasses and monument, which record that Maud Tesdale 'lovingly anointed Christ Jesus in his poore members at Glympton, Charlbury, Ascott' and elsewhere, whilst her husband was 'sober and honest in his conversation, just and upright in his dealings, bountiful in hospitality'.

Master Alexander de Langford was rector in 1237. Edward Gabet, another rector, in his will leaves 'all my syns that ever I have commited to the Devill as his owne from whome they came'.

1549. Sir Thomas Bridges and his helpers at the great pillage cleared the church of its possessions, '2 paire of vestements,' 'a coope', and '2 belles hanging in the steple.'

In 1632 the Manor consisted of '6 messuages, 2 tofts, 4 cottages, a dove house, 500 acres of land, 40 of meadow, 200 pasture, 140 wood; 20 shillings and a pound of pepper rent'. William Wheate (1633) bought the Manor, and the schedule of farm stock, etc., gives: 'One seed lipp, 1s.' 'two shoules and 3 pitch-forks 3/6.'

My great-grandmother was a housekeeper for someone at Glympton, and in her day there was an erection somewhere about there called 'Lady Wheate's Folly'. It seems to have disappeared.

During the Commonwealth the owner of Glympton complained that 'we have not had the Sacrant of ye Lords Supp for above a year past'. Another rector declined to preach, saying the congregation being small the Common Prayer would serve them well enough.

Some old accounts give items:—

'Turnpikes and beer going to Chipping Norton with 20 quarters of barley, 8/.'

'Ditto fetching home hay, 1/7½.'

'Thatching, 3/- a square.'

'Mowing 21 acres of meadow grass, £2 2s.'

'Turnpikes and beer fetching hay from Hanbro, 6/-.'

'Richard West and sons cleaning out the pond, £2 10s. Beer, 1/6. Powder and Shot, 1/4.'

'Sarah Weston spinning 7 mops, 4/1."

Hailey

This triple village, consists of

MIDDLE TOWN,

where is the church, built in 1868-9. Near-by used to stand the village stocks. A Wesleyan chapel reminds us that Methodism has had a share in the life of the place, many in its fellowship having found the 'pearl of great price'.

DELLY END

The pool reminds us how dependent is the place on surface water. A modern preaching cross is on the green, about which cluster typical Oxfordshire cottages, with the Manor House.

POFFLEY END

The Green is now allotment, and here used to be the Pound for straying cattle. Hailey had a share in the Wychwood deer in the olden days, and the keeper's house yet stands in the fields at White Oak Green towards Chase Woods Farm. The *Oxford Journal* records (June 10th, 1819):—

'The annual hunt at Chase Woods on Whit Monday was numerously attended. Capt. Freeman's hounds were thrown in to cover, and after much sport (?) four bucks were killed amidst the acclamations of the highly gratified sportsmen, who acknowledged they never saw such a day's sport before. The remainder of the day was spent in the greatest hilarity and general satisfaction prevailed.'

A quaint charity of 1649 provides money to be paid to a 'good preacher' on a certain Sunday yearly.

Crawley

This hamlet, with its setting, hill and dale, its pretty dip to the Windrush valley, is a picture. The mills remind us that we are in the famous Witney blanket country, as do the many old weaving shops where used to be hand looms. The rubbish of an old cottage here when spread on a meadow yielded a number of silver coins, some forgotten hoard, no doubt.

MAGGOTS GROVE could tell a tale could it speak. Bones, etc., found there raise questions hard to answer.

Handborough

HANEBERGE, HANEBERGAM, 1141; HAM BORROUE .

This interesting village with many spellings to its name even to-day, is in two parts, one clustering about the charming old church with its beautiful spire, and the other, 'Long', rightly so called, stretching along a Y-shaped piece of road between Woodstock and Witney. It is situated upon a strata of gravel some sixteen feet in thickness, an early deposit, at the base of which remains of elephants, etc., are found. I have teeth of these tropical animals found at Handborough.

Hanebergam in 1147 became the property of Eynsham Abbey by the gift of Leyman de Litz, in order that the souls of his parents and himself might be benefitted in the next world — so it is mentioned in the Abbey records.

Adam de Downhalle figures, 1280. Wm. Joye collected rent, 15/-, in 1325. Wm. Brownhale 1418. John Middletone 1453.

In 1370 names occur. John Smyth, John Freeman, Robt. Wilkyn, Ric. Siverston, Thos. Stillen, Walter Wynter, John Corbrigge. The rector in 1446 was Thos. Hollkyn.

Hanebergh came into the Wychwood forest perambulation in 1298, and of course had forest rights. In 1270 Queen Alimore desired to make a park of her twenty-acre wood at Haneberge, and was allowed to do so. Pigs and goats were in the forest belonging to Handborough men.

There is a pre-Reformation cross in the northern part of the churchyard. I think it is possibly the top part of a preaching or roadside cross with the stem let into the ground.

An Early English Clock

In the tower is an early clock that for centuries gave out the hours. There was no face. It is quite a museum piece, with bob pendulum and verge escapement, no doubt the work of one of our local blacksmith clock-makers.

A curious brass, with a corpse in its winding sheet, as was used generally for burials without a coffin (as were most burials formerly), tied at the head and feet and so lifted, is in the chancel, with the wording:—

'That thou art the same was y,
And thou likewise shall suer dye
Lyve so, that when thou hence welt wend
Thou maist have blys, that hath no end.
Obit Alexander Belsyre. 13 July anno domini 1567.'

He was the first president of St. John's College, Oxford, 1555, was deprived in 1562, and was not allowed to go more than two miles from Handborough, where he lived.

There are other inscriptions worth study, and on a big altar tomb in the churchyard are carved a hammer and pair of pincers.

Much interest is attached to the ancient screens and rood remains, and the modern oak seats made a few yards from the church by the parish clerk, Mr.

John Mansell, and his late son are worth notice as worthy modern craftsmanship. The weathercock on the church spire has soldered in his beak a shilling given for that purpose by an old lady who lived near.

MONEY SCALES

Traders formerly had scales to test the weight of coins. These scales were necessary as coins were clipped so much. An aged lady some years ago gave me a little set she said she had stolen when a child from her aunt's shop in Handborough.

A CROMWELLIAN BROAD

The late Mr. William Lay picked up an old book that had lain on the side wall under a roof on his property for years, and on opening it found a gold broad. He had it mounted to wear on his watch chain.

CHRIST CHURCH

There is a modern church at Long Handborough, whilst capital chapels — Wesleyan and Primitive — have done splendid work for many years as centres of religious life and activity.

Idbury

Charming exalted Idbury, set high on the hill, was within the forest long ago, and King Charles I, in 1638, has it, with Fyfield, in the list of places over which he tried to revive the old laws and restrictions, to the disgust of all true Cotswold men, who loved to be free.

The Norman builders worked at the church, making the stonework of the doorway built into the north wall. Others at later dates spent time and thought and labour over windows, bellcot with turrets carved, rood screen, bench ends cut and figured, early tombs in the churchyard, a tower with three bells, and some early craftsman long ago made a clock. The remains are in the tower, and quite worth preserving. But I think the gem of the place, if not of all our forest border, is the font. This is very beautiful, wrought, carved and moulded with thought and skill. It gives pleasure to all who behold it.

The embankments of an ancient camp show that early men saw the commanding position of the place.

Kiddington or Cuddington

Cuddington Wood is mentioned as in the Wychwood Forest in 1298, and even earlier still, in 1232, it is recorded that Thomas Decans de Barton was rector, whilst Eynsham records mention 1148-61 Reginaldo de Cudintone. The history of the place by Warton is well known. The church, with its abundance of ball flower ornament, brass to Walter Goodere, stone to Clement, the King's armourer, in the floor, the quaint, finely cut gravestones in the churchyard, the ancient pillars in front of the mansion close at hand, with the remains of the ancient village cross, all make this place one to linger long in the memory.

Then it is recorded that long ago, one was re-baptised in the church for profane swearing. Our fathers did things well as they thought, was it morals or other things, when they set about it. The dovecote close to the church, in the grounds of Kiddington Hall, surmounted by a dove in lead, must not be forgotten.

PAINTED GLASS.—The windows of Cherrington Church, in Warwickshire, are aglow with painted glass placed there by a late rector, Rev. Dr. Warner. Some of it was taken from windows in the old mansion at Kiddington about the year 1750.

ARMOUR.—Formerly there were some helmets within the church, but they have gone. This is a pity.

There is a story told of a waggon, horses and man, being completely engulfed in Moor Lake, only the ploughboy escaping to tell the tale.

The following verses by the late George Busby, of Kiddington, are of interest:—

THE WORCESTERBURY

Like a waif from some distant wreckage
  So borne o'er the wreck of Time,
Lives a name, with a story clinging
  At this village on the Glyme.

Down through eleven centuries,
  While much has been forgot,
This old name, Worcesterbury,
  Still lingers round the spot.

It tells of days when Offa,
  As King of Mercia reigned:
From the monks of Worcester
  Here gift of land obtained.

'Twould seem some of their Order
  Soon came to found a cell;
A bury, the Saxons called it,
  Where they designed to dwell.

Sad that their new-made garden,

Wherein they often toiled,
And all good work accomplished,
  So soon should be despoiled.

Scarce time here for disclosing
  The sweets of Sharon's rose,
To cheer these wilds so dreary
  Ere came wide spreading woes.

Not long to raise their voices
  To heaven, in prayer and praise,
Before the Danes were on them,
  Who soon their home did raize.

As they had served Medeshampstead,
  And many a place beside,
Slain true folk at Hook Norton
  So, at our countryside.

The Worcesterbury they plundered,
  The monks, 'twould seem, were slain;
And thus, our native village,
  Did in their hands remain.

A Danish chieftain, Clapa,
  His name we seem to trace
In Clapyatt, where, a hillfort,
  Time doth not quite erase.

The Worcesterbury in ruins,
  The Saxons' homes laid low,
What scenes of desolation!
  Near where our Glyme doth flow.

Since days of Danes and Saxons,
  Through changes in this place,
The name has been remembered
  Here, by the village race.

On down through all the centuries,
  A thousand years and more,
It lingers yet to tell the tale
  Of deeds in days of yore.

Langley

In 1533, Leland records:— 'rode 3 or 4 miles through Wichwood longinge to the Kynge where is plenty of wood and fallow deer. … Langley a myle from Burford there remayne tokens of an old Manor Place in the syde of the forest.'

There was a glory, past in Leland's day, a ruin possibly made habitable again. Some years ago I used to go by the footway from Fair Spear across close to Langley house every Monday morning about six-thirty, coming back on Saturdays. This I did for over a year, so I saw a good bit of it and the house as it is. The old boundary wall is very ancient, a stone door-head used to lie just by the road side. Report always connects King John with the place, but strange to say there seems no documentary evidence to show that he ever was there. His forester, Thomas de Langley, no doubt resided there.

In 1213 he gave King John 100 marks and a palfrey to have the custody of the forest of Wychwode. A mark, 13/4, would now be about £16, so Thomas must have had a long stocking up the chimney somewhere.

The present house with carved initials H. & E. with the Tudor rose in relief, are of much later date, and are thought to be those of Henry VII and his Queen.

There used to lie at a cottage door here at Charlbury a fine old gargoyle, and on enquiry I found that it was pulled out of the pool at Langley by members of the family in whose possession it then was. They prized it greatly, so my designs for getting it came to nothing. However, I saw it with much interest, especially when I knew its history.

The de Langley family were of great account in all the forest district. They erected the Langley Mill, on the Evenlode between Shipton and Ascott. Most of the other mills are so ancient that their origin is lost in the mists of the past.

Wm. Est, freemason, is paid £9 for repairs at Woodstock and Langley in 1516, and again in 1518.

Henry VIII seems to have favoured Langley as a place of residence, many notices of his being there occurring in State documents of 1526. In 1529 a letter to Cardinal Wolsey mentions his presence there. Anne Bolyn was there too. She writes a letter dated from Langley and signed 'Your loving mestress Anne the Quene'.

In 1536 Sir John and Thomas Bridges have the keeping of Langley and Minster Lovell, Burford, Shipton, Spellsbury, the bailiwick of Chadlington and the eight walks in Wychwood Forest.

Later, Earl Leicester had Langley in his charge, and Elizabeth went through Burford from Langley.

Perhaps all do not know the rhyme —

'Our good Queen Bess, she made a pudden,
And stuffed it full o' plums;
And in she put gret dabs o' fat
As big as my two thumbs.'

Some years ago an old hunting knife was found under the boards of an old cottage window at Langley.

After the Restoration in 1660 King Charles II gave to Earl Clarendon 'Langley, Leefield and Ramsden'. It had belonged to Lord Danvers, who died at Cornbury in 1643.

Lord Danvers was noted for his hospitality, the overflowing abundance of which looks attractive to this day. Any hungry man or woman who could get to Cornbury in his day soon found cause to rejoice.

A chapel was to be built there in an acre of ground granted for that purpose in 1230. Nutteridge is considered to be the site.

In 1306 John de Langley's right to the manor was challenged, but his claim was established.

Warton in 1815 speaks of the ruins of Langley. To-day it is the site of a wonderful ten-mast wireless receiving station controlled by the Postmaster-General.

Leafield

LA FELD, 1298.

Most commonly called by the working people 'Field Town', is also given that name in the Pottery Handbook issued by the British Museum. 'The Village in the Fields' gets its name because of its isolation, no main road being near it.

I have heard that not so many years ago, before the enclosures and the road were made, that after dark it was a most adventurous journey to get from Finstock over the heath to Leafield. Perhaps pits, ditches, briars, ruts, etc., to be encountered if you ever did get across.

Two things strike one forcibly at the village. First, the splendid prospect, a view over many counties, wonderful to see. Second, the lack (till recently) of water in summer. Fancy having to go with yoke and buckets down to the spring 'Uz-zell' right away in the forest, for drinking water, or else buy from a man with a water cart in the street!

This drawback has at last been overcome by the gift of a spring of water near Shipton by Mr. J. F. Maddox. This, under the skilful guidance of Mr. A. T. Green (surveyor), has been sent up to the village. In July, 1927, the formal opening took place, the water being turned on by the lord of the manor, who, with others, had made the scheme possible. There were present members of the Rural District Council (chairman, Mr. Blair). Prayer was offered bvy the Vicar Rev. Balfour, and the hymn, 'Now thank we all our God' was heartily sung after which Mr. N. Parsons spoke. He was followed bv Mr. Watney, who referred to the long barrow men, the Celts, and so on down. All these, and their descendants, had suffered from the lack of water, but at any rate Leafield had its water supply now. An illuminated address was presented to Mr. Maddox, bearing the names: N. F. W. Balfour, G. Gordon, E. W. Holloway, W. Dore, A. W. Perkins, T. Hewett, C. Baker. The planting of an oak tree was followed by a tea. Then an inspection of the works brought to a close an epoch-marking day.

HIGH BARROW

On the highest point is an ancient barrow 320 feet in circumference and some eleven feet in height, known locally as 'Barry Hill Tump'. This, and the trees and steeple near, are a landmark from far away.

Before 1860 Leafield was one of the many places in Shipton civil parish.

THE CROSS

The Cross, restored in 1873, has an ancient base.

THE CHURCH

A church was built in 1590 by Sir Henry Unton. Another replaced it in 1822, whilst the present fine structure to St. Michael and All Angels, by Street, was built in 1860.

A newspaper cutting, November, 1877:—

'The new bells rang out a merry peal for upwards of half an hour; this is the first time the ringers—all new hands at their work—have rung except in practice.'

In the year 1926 there were six burials, the youngest person buried being 80 and the oldest 90. One old lady buried in February, 1927, at the age of 86, had, it is thought, never been further away from Leafield than to Woodstock (ten miles). This journey was accomplished in a farm waggon. It is thought that her only ride in a train was when the line was opened from Ascott to Shipton.

A Baptist chapel, with manse, is at the west end of the Green. 'A tablet within bears an inscription: 'This tablet was erected by the family of the late Robert Abraham, of Ringwood, Minster Lovel, in memory of their father, who in the year 1883 (?) gave this Chapel, Manse, and adjoining buildings for the worship of God by Protestant Dissenters.'

POTTERY

The art of the potter has been in evidence at Leafield down to recent times. The discovery of pottery and earthenware in the graves of pre-historic man gives an idea how ancient is this art. Vessels, hand made, not turned on a wheel but moulded into shape by the fingers, funeral urns and drinking vessels of coarse clay imperfectly burnt are found in our pre-Roman barrows and tombs. The use of the potter's wheel is thought to have been unknown here before the second century B.C. but this may not be correct. Specimens of turned vessels are found, but they may have been imported from elsewhere.

Many fragments of both red and black pottery lie in the soil about the long barrow at Slate Pits Copse in Wychwood Forest which show evidence of their having been turned on a wheel.

These early men believed in the continuity of life, as they placed vessels of food about their dead. Perhaps they knew more than we think they did. Do we moderns believe as simply and as surely as they. That they looked forward to a life beyond this present these barrows and their contents tell us plainly.

After the Roman conquest the art of the Continental potter was brought here, and our clay was moulded into beautiful shapes. Slip patterns and glaze were used. During the dark days that followed the Roman period most things requiring taste and skill seemed to come to an end, and for long it is uncertain what the potter did. Nearer our day, however, he became busy again, and vessels of burnt clay have been in constant demand, and bricks, etc., were made at many places.

Field Town, fixed on as a site for a barrow and a dwelling place because of its splendid commanding position, had clay in abundance ready to hand to make vessels for the village and countryside.

The name 'Potter's Hill' and the village inn, 'The Potter's Arms', still suggest the craft which formerly flourished there.

Franklin is a name long connected with the local clay work, bricks and pottery. When I was a lad I used to watch 'Cutter Franklin', as he was called, and his son skilfully make pots, pans, etc., on the wheel at the pottery on the left hand side of the road just a little beyond the Baptist chapel on the Shipton Road. They have both passed away, and there seems to be no other to carry on the work.

There was formerly another pottery nearer the village on the other side of the road.

Many gifts and qualities were needed by a potter I could see. Great care in selecting and preparing the clay; knowledge, care and skill to work at the wheel to make vessels true to shape and size; moulding and fixing handles; glazing and firing — the latter a most responsible job, for which, I believe, one or two nights had to be spent at the furnace to see all was well. To be a potter a man had to give him self to his job in down right earnest.

Hawkers used to travel the neighbourhood with this 'Field Town Cha'ney', and it is a great pity that the craft of the potter has ended at Leafield.

CLAY PIPES

Not long ago I saw the remains of one of the furnaces where tobacco pipes used to be burnt at Leafield, and I remember as a lad a man who was a tobacco pipe maker. He was, I should say, the last to do anything at this craft in our district.

I asked an old friend of mine from Finstock at the market here a time ago, what was the pipe maker's name. He at once replied, 'Old Gooseberry'. Yes, I said, but what was his name? Again he gave the same reply, and soon it dawned on him what I wished to know was not his nick name. With a smile he said he never knew him by any other name than 'Old Gooseberry'.

THE STOCKS

Law and order were kept as at other places by a constable, with stocks to confine and punish the unruly. At some places when a man was confined in the Stocks he had many sympathising friends. They would bring drink to him, as he sat in them, and often his last state was worse than his first.

The last man to be placed in Leafield stocks seems to have been a man of resource. He sent a lad for a saw, and as he sat there he cut himself out and the stocks were never repaired. The ironwork went to the blacksmith, and I bought from him the big, strong hasp by which the stocks were fastened.

Milton-under-Wychwood

MIDDLETONE, 1086.

A corruption of 'Middle Town', it is said. Wychwood gives its sheltering name to distinguish it from other Miltons in the county. That it is needed the following will show. Years ago I was at a meeting in the schoolroom, and as the speaker billed did not turn up a local man, Mr. J. Couling, stepped into the breach and took us, as he was well able, into the exalted places where are crowns and a 'great white throne'. At length the door opened and the lecturer came in. The late Mr. Alfred Groves who was my neighbour, said — referring to what we had heard — 'he will have a job to better it'. Mr. John Jasper commenced his speech by saying: 'All the address given me was "Miss Groves, The Elms, Milton", and this is the third Milton I have been at to-day.'

THE CHURCH

The church is nicely situated, and is a good building in the Decorated style. It was built in 1854, at the cost chiefly of Mr. J. H. Langston.

The Green, which is fenced in, is much appreciated and well used for gatherings and games. Quite an historic meeting, addressed by the late Joseph Arch, was held there in the seventies.

Considerable charities of coal and bread show that there was kindly thought towards Milton long ago.

Quakers and Baptists at Milton

There was a Quaker meeting established at Milton and a meeting house built. Here earnest souls met and found, doubtless, Him who comes to those who meet in His name.

'And not for signs in heaven above
    Or earth below they look,
Who know with John His smile of love,
    With Peter His rebuke.
In inward peace, or sense
    Of sorrow over sin,
He is His own best evidence;
    His witness is within.'

It appears that in the nineteenth century sin and ignorance prevailed pretty largely at Milton. God's day was profaned and given over to prize-fighting, bull baiting, and all ungodliness. Two good women, Mrs. Green and Miss Upstone, were led to confer with a Mr. Pool, of Ascott, and John Turner, of Pudlicote, and at Mr. Pill's house at Upper Milton a religious service was started, being held at eight o'clock on Sunday mornings. A Baptist minister from Burford, the Rev. J. Smith, conducted it. The rough element did all they could to oppose it. Stones were thrown at the door, and more than once the stream was diverted to run into the house, 'to give the dippers plenty of water', it was said. However, the work continued, and 1808 a Mr. Goffe, of Hook Norton, built a chapel. Two years later a division took place. But again the cause rallied, under the ministry of the Rev. John Hirons, assisted by the Rev. T. Edens. Other men have carried on, and amongst them the Rev. G. W. Davidson, of fragrant memory, must have mention.

The Particular, or Strict, Baptists

Dec. 5th, 1841,

We, whose names are hereafter mentioned, do unanimously consent and agree in the presence of the Lord and each other to form ourselves into a society meeting together for Divine worship in Zoar Chapel, Milton.

GEORGE GORTON, Pastor.   WILLIAM HAWKES.
SARAH BARNES.   ELIZA HAWKES.

This cause continues, and all down the years has been a centre for worship and fellowship for many earnest, godly souls.

Methodism

Primitive Methodism got a strong footing at Milton. A chapel was built and glorious camp meetings were held upon the Green. The late Mr. Isaac Castle was a tower of strength. His tent was a feature for all good work, both religious and temperance, and he built a house with a room for a coffee tavern, so that there should be somewhere besides the public house as a place of call and refreshment. There can be no doubt that he strove most earnestly to help his fellows. Wesleyan Methodism became established, I believe, as the result of a young man, Mr. Mills, preaching. A chapel was built, and later, services were held in a mission room. Burwel, Miles, Pratley, and Williams are names which will long be remembered as Methodists at Milton.

A WYCHWOOD BUILDER

Milton owes much to the fact that the late Mr. Alfred Groves conducted an extensive building business there, which is still continued by his sons at the village. He was a remarkable man. His knowledge of the art of building, coupled with gifts and qualities of a high order, a keen sense of humour, and a great love for little children, made him quite a man above the average. I have many pleasant memories of him. One of the earliest is of one day when I was going to school up the Well Hill, Finstock. Mr. Groves was going the same way. I knew who he was — indeed, his fine commanding presence and his tall white hat made him so conspicuous that once seen he was never to be forgotten. He said, 'Well, little boy; going to school?' I said 'Yes, sir.' (We were taught in those days to be respectful to those older than ourselves.) He gave me a penny and said, 'Do you know your pence tables?' I said I did, but, as will be seen, this soon got me into trouble, showing up my ignorance, as at once he said, 'How much is a hundred pence?' I replied, 'Five shillings.' He said, 'I don't think it is.' But that was all I could do. Before we parted at the school he put me right and gave me a sixpence — I think perhaps the first whole sixpence I had ever had. Many busy, happy hours I spent afterwards in his company. With a face like the Sphinx he would ask questions quite beyond my ken. I respect his memory, and with other Milton folk he has a warm place in my heart. Through his business, work came from all the Forest district, and beyond.

Minster Lovell

MINISTRE, 1110.

Roger de Chesney gave to Eynsham Abbey the tithe of his land in 'Ministre' before 1110. The second name Lovel, is said to have had its origin in a nickname Lupelles, which got tacked on to the son of Robert, who came over with the Conqueror. It got shortened to Lupel, then to Luvel or Lovel. The family owned two mills at Minister in 1197.

About 1200 Maud, wife of William Lovell, gave the church to a foreign religious house, who instituted a clerk, Henry by name.

In 1239 it is spoken of in the Eynsham records as the tithe of a hide of land called Murdakshide, worth in 1254 6/8, and in 1270 worth 10/-. Later this passed, perhaps by exchange, to Eton.

An inquisition in 1292 states John Lovell had a wood within the cover of Whichwood, also half the water of the Winrisse (Windrush) from Wolmaresham bridge to Minster Mill. In 1425 William Lovell was granted liberty to impark Minster woods and two fields. About this date the second name was added, making Minster Lovell, as to-day.

In 1437 that plucky lady, who was maid of honour to the queen of James I of Scotland, and who, when the assassins came to murder the king, thrust her arm into the door staple, the bar having been taken away, and whose arm was broken when the door was forced, became the wife of Sir Richard Lovell. Collingbourn was executed for making the rhyme re the King, Sir Richard Ratcliffe, Sir W. Catesby and Lord Lovell:—

'The cat, the rat, and Lovell our dogge,
Rule all England under an hogge.'

At Bosworth field Lovell got away and escaped to Ireland, coming back to fight at Stoke. His fate after that is not known with certainty. A story of his skeleton being found in a vault at Minster is a fancy, I should say.

These lines were on a tablet at Haliwell:—

'All ye nuns of Haliwell,
Pray ye both day and night
For the soul of Sir Thomas Lovel,
Whom Harry the seventh made knight.'

THE RUINS

The mansion is glorious in its ruinous state, and must have been magnificent in its prime. From the ground covered by the ruins it is easy to see the proportions of this ancient dwelling. It stood in a delightful spot, though, according to modern ideas, too near to the river. Dense forest, 'Wychwood', was about it in early days, and all the beasts of the chase were at its very doors. The castle, as some call it, is said to have been the scene of the tragic story 'The Mistletoe Bough' — the young bride who hid in the chest with a spring lock, and could not be found until, long long after, on its being opened, 'a skeleton lay mouldering there'.

The church, close to the mansion, is a very complete example of the Perpendicular style, and is worth close examination. The tomb with effigy is ascribed to various Lovells, but no one seems able to fix with certainty which out of three it commemorates.

THE DOVE HOUSE

The fine old dovecot is a splendid specimen, and I cannot understand why, with all that has been written of this place, no notice has been taken of this building. It is circular in form, with multitudes of nesting places built in the thickness of the wall inside, all round the place from top to bottom. The ladder that used to revolve with a frame on a central pivot has gone.

When an old turning lathe flywheel was taken (or fell) to pieces at the carpenter's shop not far away, it was found to be an old millstone, mounted and boxed in as a wheel.

Away on the hill to the left is what is locally known as the Estate or 'Lot-tees', where are many detached houses of similar design, mostly of one storey. This is one of the estates laid out in 1849 by the Chartist Land Company. Excellent as may have been the intention, it was forgotten that not all men possess the many gifts and talents necessary to make a living from a plot of land. That these gifts are not universal many a townsman has learnt to his sorrow.

THE MINSTER LOVELL JEWEL

The West Saxon kings appear to have had great treasures of gold. About 715 King Ina's chapel contained an altar of gold weighing 264 lbs. The chalice and paten, of the same metal, weighed 10 lbs. In addition to other golden articles, the structure contained silver to the tune of 2,640 lbs., and altogether it must have been a gorgeous place. King Alfred's jewel, in the Ashmolean Museum, is well known, but a very similar piece of goldsmith's work, close to it in the same case, is not so well known. This was found at Minster Lovell, and is of interest to all lovers of the Wychwood country as a local relic of those Anglo-Saxon days, and of fine goldsmith's artistry.

I have been told of an old silver spoon found at or near the ruins, but it was disposed of before I got on the track of it.

Northleigh

NORTHLEYE. NORTHLEGH.

The grey old tower could tell us many things if it could speak. We will look at it and think, and we may find something of its story. It looks as though Saxon masons prepared the baulaster windows, and that later men prepared the arches and built the tower, using the stonework that earlier workers had got ready. Does the blocked-up west arch, with the inserted tie beams in the tower, covered with artful little slate-covered dormers where they are keyed outside, mean that there was a settlement in early days and the nave taken down at the west, and built at the east, as to-day? The jacket of plaster is dated 1740.

John de St. John gave the church to Eynsham Abbey about 1150.

In 1225 Robert, Count of Dreux, possessed the patronage of the church. The gem of the building is the Wilcote chantry chapel, in beautiful Perpendicular style; and charming indeed it is — a splendid legacy from the days of long ago, giving joy to all who see it. Some old glass is in the traceried windows and there is fan traceried vaulting overhead.

Fan Vaulting. Left: Northleigh, Wilcote Chapel. Right: Burford Church porch

It is the setting for an altar tomb which stands underneath an ogee arch inserted between the chapel and the chancel. This tomb is that of Elizabeth Blackett and her first husband, Sir William Wilcotes, who died in 1411. The Wilcote arms are on the helmet on which his head rests. His two sons, with their mother, applied for a licence to found the chantry in 1440. The beautiful figures are not fixed, and they do not correspond in size. This suggests that Sir William's effigy was placed first on the centre of the tomb and was moved later to make room for that of his wife — perhaps at her death. She is represented in what was then old-fashioned dress, and one can fancy her children telling the sculptor, 'Mother must be dressed as she was — as we knew and loved her.' Her arms appear, 'a chevron invecked (that is, an object like a pair of rafters, with hollow shaped notches in them) and three scallop shells.' Some details are well preserved.

WHITEWASH

Rawlinson, the antiquary, said of one church: 'This church may in a manner be said to have been rebuilt, she having repaired it in the most beautiful manner by white washing.' My grandfather had a standing order from Mrs. Castle, the lady at Northleigh Grange, as Wilcote House used to be called, to whitewash this chapel once a year. In 1864 Thomas Smith and my father scraped off all the whitewash, leaving the stonework as it is to-day.

The names of the Martin family (one of whom built what is called Finstock Manor House in 1660) are in the floor. John and Thomas Martin, and also Jas. Perrott, of Northleigh, are names in the deeds of Charlbury Grammar School, 1685.

THE BUCKINGHAM BRASS

This brass in the chancel floor to Thomas Buckingham, 1431, has more than one story. Here is one:

A fearful monster, the terror of all men, was in Fish-hill Bottom. Buckingham came home from the wars on furlough and hearing, of course, of this dread reptile, dragon, or monster, resolved to do battle with it. Taking his sword he went alone — terror keeping spectators away — to meet this vile thing. He succeeded in killing it, but in doing so lost his own life. They were found in the morning lying dead—he with his feet upon the monster, as depicted on the brass.

Another and more recent story was told me by the late Vicar, the Rev. Scott.

Three men one day asked for the key of the church, and as after a considerable time they did not return with it he (Mr. Scott) thought he would go and see what had happened. To his surprise he found the door locked and the men inside the church. As the old pipe key could only be used to lock the door from the outside, it was evident they had gone out by the north door and locked the south door, afterwards re-entering by the north door which they shut and barred. On going round Mr. Scott found this to be the case, and that he was locked and barred out of his own church! Presently the key was brought back and nothing amiss was discovered. On Sunday morning, however, the organist found that the organ had been moved bodily. This had been upon the Buckingham brass. No doubt some rubbings had been taken, but this was not the nicest way to get them.

Beautiful tablets are on the walls. The names on some of them arrest us. 'Lenthall', 'Musgrave', and 'Perrott' are there.

Over the chancel arch are wall paintings. In the churchyard there are an abundance of headstones, many from stone formerly dug in the parish at East End. Many of these, with fine carving, were cut by the father of the late Mr. George Lord.

Away on the hill is the windmill ruin. It was built by the late Mr. Shepherd not so long ago. A story is told that someone stole a bag of money belonging to him, and the thief could not be discovered. On Mr. Shepherd going out one day to Banbury, or some distant place, it got put about that he was gone to consult the 'Cunning Man' as to who was the thief. This story, though it was not true, seems to have scared the guilty party, for on some haycocks in the Windmill Field being turned, the stolen bag, with the contents untouched, was discovered.

NORTHLEIGH TOKEN

I have a specimen, as follows:—

Obverse: WILLIAM . AND . ANN= Three letters on a central heart device, w . A . M .
Reverse: MASON . IN . NORTHLY   THEIR HALF PENY.

Note the spelling.

ASHFORD MILL

Ashford Mill, in Northleigh parish, figures in a nursery rhyme that dates back to Charles II, 1660:

'Lucy Locket lost her pocket,
  Kitty Fisher found it,
Took it down to Ashford Mill,
  And Ashford miller ground it.'

THE ROMAN VILLA

About 1813 in a field called Roman Piece, about a mile from the church, near the river, walls and tesselated pavements were discovered. They had been noticed some years before, but with not so much interest as to cause extensive excavation. It is considered to have been a villa of good size, and must have been the residence of some important person, maybe a Romanised Briton. Many coins were found, Cladius, Carausius, Allectus, Constantius, etc., etc. A piece of the floor uncovered has been roofed in, and the Roman system of heating can be seen. Many fragments of stone will be noticed.

It appears to have been overwhelmed in utter destruction, and no doubt served as a quarry for materials for all the near neighbourhood. A marble bath from the villa found its way into an orchard at Handborough. How, I do not know, and perhaps it would be better to ask no questions. There it lay in the stinging nettles until one day someone saw it who recognised its value. He purchased it from my friend, on whose ground it lay, for five pounds, and it was conveyed to Dumfries Museum, where, I daresay, it can yet be seen.

March 21st, 1761, *Jackson's Oxford Journal* records the sending of 140 men of the Militia to quell any attempts that may be made to destroy the fences of the new enclosures on North Leigh Heath. Much resentment seems to be nursed to-day against the attempt being made to enclose more of the ancient common.

'THESE LITTLE ONES'

Some years ago three little children, two girls and a boy, wandered off into the fields between East End and Coombe and got lost. Night came, and as they were utterly worn out they gave it up, and in a field of barley knelt down and said their prayers, and then lay down and slept. Some time in the night the boy, who was, I believe, the smallest of the three, awoke and complained how cold he was. A hue and cry was raised, of course, over these precious little people, and in the morning they were found by a gamekeeper, none the worse for their adventure.

TELL ME ANOTHER

Shortly after the death of George III it is said a lady of some means sent her servant to the 'Leather Bottel' public house with a sovereign, to get change. The girl came back with nineteen shillings, saying: 'This is all they would give me, seeing it is the old King's money.' Her mistress said: 'What a pity, seeing I have so many of them.'

Ramsden

Ramsden was an early settlement on an ancient track or saltway which the Romans covered in their day by a part of Akeman Street. The pools of water that never fail were a water supply in the absence of a stream. The pool at Skippet is a good-sized pond.

In 1292 one Nicholas of Ramsden was fined half a mark for poaching in the forest.

In 1414 James of Ramsden was made Abbot of Eynsham Abbey. He wrote the bishop, it is recorded, about Abbey matters in 1417. He was living in 1429. Not much seems to be known about him.

Ramsden was formerly in Shipton parish, so weddings and funerals took place there. The church was built in 1872 by the late Rev. R. Lowbridge Baker, in memory of his first wife.

There is a Wesleyan chapel, in connection with which an annual camp meeting has been held without a break from beyond living memory.

The words along the wall of one Ramsden cottage, just below the eaves, 'MARY'S COTTAGE', are very remarkable. I think they are wrought iron. They are well formed Roman letters, but nothing seems to be known about them.

Wilcote Lane used to continue further, where is now only a foot way, and in a wide part in days past 'single stick' and 'kick shin' encounters used to take place on Sunday mornings. I wonder if there was any connection between the age-long disagreement between Finstock and Ramsden boys (which I hope has now gone for ever) and these Sunday morning encounters.

The Manor House, 'The Old Hall', with its big porch, is worth notice. It is now the residence of Lord Olivier.

EDWARD LEECH AND WILLIAM ROBBERDES

To all Christian people to whom this present writing shall come down to be seen, read, heard, or understood I, EDWARD LEECH of RAMSDEN, in the county OXON, labourer, send greeting in our Lord God everlasting.

Know ye that I the said Edward Leech for and in consideration of the sum of forty shillings of lawful English money to me in hand paid by WILLIAM ROBBERDES of Ramsden aforesaid woolman, before the ensealing and delivery hereof and in consideration that he the said Wm. Robberdes did by his deed poll bearing the date hereof give grant bargain sell assign and set over unto me the said Edward Leech one indenture of lease bearing date the 17th day of September in the seventh year of the reign of our late Sovereign Lord King James of England made by one THOMAS LARDNER of Ramsden aforesaid husband man unto one WILLIAM THACKERAY of FAWLER in the said county shepherd of one messuage or tenement built and erected in a parcel of ground in Ramsden aforesaid called HOGGE HEYES, and of other lands and things in the same indenture specified for the term of one & thirty years beginning from the feast of the purifications of the Blessed Virgin St. Mary in the year of our LORD GOD 1613 for the yearly rent of 4/- to have and to hold the said indenture of lease & the premises thereby demised unto me the said Edward Leech my executors administrators and assigns for and during all the residue then to come and unexpired of the said term of one and thirty years which indenture of lease I have received together with the said 40/- have granted enfeofft released and confirmed and by these presents do fully and absolutely for and in my heirs grant bargain sell release enfeofft and confirm unto the said William Robberdes all that my cottage or tenement with the garden and backside belonging situate lying and being in Ramsden aforesaid next between the tenement of JOHN BISHOP on the one side and JOHN LEE on the other side and late in the possession of Thomas Leech my father deceased and sithence in the possesion & occupation of me the said Edward & now in the occupation of the said Wm. Robberdes together with all the commons herbage & appurtenances thereunto belonging or appertaining to have & to hold the said cottage or tenement & all other the said granted premises with the appurtenances unto the said Wm. Robberdes his heirs & assigns to the only sole and proper use & behoof of him the said Wm. Robberdes his heirs & assigns for ever & I the said Edward Leech & my heirs all the said cottage or tenement and other the above granted premises with the appurtenances unto the said Wm. Robberdes his heirs & assigns for the yearly rent of 8d. payable to me my heirs or assigns on the Feasts of the

Annunciation of our Blessed Lady St. Mary the Virgin St. Michael the Archangel by equal portions being parcel of the quit rent of 16d. payable to the said John Lee, for & out of the premises & for other lands which I hold to me & my heirs against me the said Edward Leech & against Alice my wife will for ever warrant & defend by these presents…

In witness whereof I the said Edward Leech have here unto set my hand and seal Dated the 10th day of November in the 10th year of the Reign of our Sovereign Lord Charles by the Grace of God King of England Scotland France & Ireland Defender of the Faith etc. Sealed and delivered in the presence of   Signed,
                                             EDWARD LEECH.

GEORGE BOX X (his mark)
TIMOTHY BROOME (?)

The above is part of a Ramsden deed (in Latin) belonging to Mrs. S. J. Shilson, translated by Miss M. Hollings.

Shipton-under-Wychwood

This ancient village, pleasantly situated on the Evenlode, has a varied story. In Doomsday 'Sciptone and Swinbroc, 4½ hides'.

The name seems to mean the Sheep Town. ' Sheep' is 'Ship' in dialect to-day. Years ago a man told me he was working in London, and saw a sheep being brought down the street to a butchers', and going into the building where he was employed said to a workman 'There is a ship just coming down the street.' The man looked up in astonishment and exclaimed 'Never; can't be.'

Geoffrey de Cruce and John Belet were early names. A mansion belonged to the Algars. Hugh de Spencer had it in Edward III's day; later Alan de Zouch, then his daughter, Maud, wife of Robert Holland.

Later the Lovells had it till they forfeited it, and Henry VII gave it to Jaspar, Duke of Bedford. Presently it got into the hands of the Beauchamps, Earls of Warwick.

Lacys built the Court in Elizabeth's day, and in 1746 Sir Compton Reade bought the place. The Reades were men of affairs. Sir Robert was Chief Justice, and several served as Sheriffs.

THE CHURCH

Shipton Church has much of interest and is well known. Its spire has a rather cumbrous capstone, and figures are carved sprawling on top of dormers, with originally a cross on each figure's head. There is a big slate clock face all may see, and the doorway beneath is of rich design. The south porch has niches with figures, the Annunciation being on one side. The font has carved panels, 'the bear and ragged staff' being on one. The stone pulpit is very interesting, and is unusual in our district. Is there another original stone pulpit, save at Coombe, in all the forest border? Another feature worth notice is the stone figure in the recess at the base of the north wall. In the corner near by, hinged to the wall, is a brass. See both sides. Beautiful tablets are on the walls. The original keys of the church hang overhead in the vestry off the chancel. They were discovered buried, having been hidden or lost long ago.

Several votive crosses are on the left-hand side of the south doorway.

Skelton records seeing a quaint stone in the church wall with garter carved bearing the words 'Richard Foxe built this window, 1548'. I saw it for sale not long since at Oxford. John Foxe, author of 'The Book of Martyrs', lived at Shipton at one time it is said.

WILLIAM LANGLAND

One of the great figures in English literature, William Langland (1330-1400?) is said to have been born at Shipton, of which place his father was a native, though little is known about him. Educated and assisted by patrons, whose death left him poor, he had to support a not very congenial wife by singing masses for the dead and other not very profitable work. At London, where he found himself, his heart came this way to the hills and fields between here and Malvern, which he knew in his youth, and he saw 'in a somer season when soft was the sonne', the great vision of a 'faire felde ful of folke', saw the doom of all insincere and purposeless lives and the glory of truth and work, and so 'The Vision of Piers Plowman' came into being.

EXTENT OF THE PARISH

Several places formerly were in this parish. Leafield, Ramsden, Milton, Lyneham, and Langley all buried at Shipton. This seems strange to-day, but the clergy, naturally, welcomed all fees, and burials and weddings brought money which was no doubt very welcome. A curious big two-storied tomb should be noticed at the east end. On one headstone is carved a hand holding, it is said, a pound of butter, and on the opposite side another hand with a pound of candles. No doubt it had some meaning with reference to the person buried there, but that is now lost.

My grandmother was present at a wedding of someone from Ramsden long ago. Later on some law case came on connected with this wedding, and grandmother had to go to London to give evidence, riding in an open-top railway carriage.

There is the old tale of the Ramsden corpse getting lost under the snow whilst the bearers were squirrel hunting at Five Ash Bottom.

A friend told me recently that his grandmother went with a burial party which, for some reason, had to get another horse in the forest. Whilst waiting for it to be brought the men of the party went for a rabbit hunt.

A MAN TRAP

When I first went to Shipton as a lad there was a board on a wall opposite the gas works with the warning words 'Man Trap' upon it. Since 1828 it has been an offence punishable by five years penal servitude to set one of these out of doors. They can be used within a dwelling house for burglars to-day.

SEVENTEENTH CENTURY TOKEN

Obverse: JOHN . WELLS . OF . SHIPTON= The Grocers' Arms
Reverse: VNDER . WITCHWOOD= I . D . W .

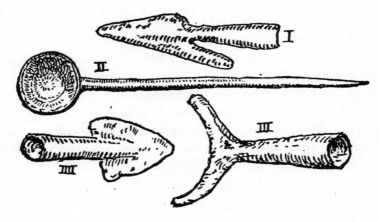

*I.–Broken arrowhead found in Charlbury.   II.–Snail Spoon.   III.–Poacher's arrowhead.
IIII.–Arrowhead from Swinbrook meadows.*

A ROMAN SNAIL SPOON

When the excavations for the Leafield water works were in progress at Shipton a Roman snail spoon, called a *cochlea* (a snail), was dug up far below the surface. They were usually of bronze, but this is silver. It has a circular bowl with a slender pointed stem, the point being well adapted for extracting snails, whelks, etc., of which the Romans were very fond, from their shells. It was also used for eating eggs.

Southleigh

SUTTHUN ET LEYE, 1264-68.

Two things have brought fame to this little village of elm trees and deep ditches and have made it the Mecca of many pilgrims.

One is that on October 16th, 1725 a keen, polished, newly ordained deacon of the Church of England preached his first sermon there. The second is that at the church restoration in 1872 some remarkable wall paintings were discovered under the whitewash.

The preacher was John Wesley, the son of a clergyman with some Puritan blood in his veins, who became the leader of the Methodist movement, which has had untold influence on the whole world. At the restoration the pulpit got put into the churchyard, and the Methodists enquired if it was for sale. The vicar said 'he had too much respect for John Wesley to sell it', so John Miles, a mason I knew later on, cut a new stone base, and on that it was set up as seen to-day. The pulpit and pews were given to the church in 1712 by John Gore.

A brass on the pulpit records Wesley's famous saying that he 'lived and died a member of the Church of England'. Yet he had led an organisation practically outside the pale of that church, organised on an independent basis, even publishing a Prayer Book for its use. I recently bought a copy on a penny shelf at Oxford, formerly the property of a Margaret Allen, of High Wycombe.

At the Bicentenary Service held in the village chapel, conducted by the Rev. Dr. Ferrier Hulme (the present vicar thought it best not to have any service within the church), after the service I had the pleasure of seeing Wesley's sermon manuscript yet preserved, which he preached two hundred years previously at Southleigh. The secret of his great effectiveness lay in the experience he had in Aldersgate Street, London, at a meeting on May 24th, 1738. This never left him. Before this he was 'weak and as another man'; after, his word was mighty and prevailed.

At the restoration of the church the Royal Arms were taken away, also an old hatchment on the right of the chancel arch, and a brass, 1557, in the floor got fixed to the south wall.

The Rev. Gerard Moultrie, who was vicar in 1869, was the author of 'Six Years' Work at Southleigh' (1875). He was also the author and translator of many hymns.

There are some interesting screens in the church. The glass formerly in the east window got blown out, I heard. This was a pity. The clock, with its apt face wording, 'It is time to seek the Lord', was put in by a former clergyman, the Rev. East, who was skilled in horology.

A curious quern, or hand-mill for grinding corn, is in the University Museum at Oxford. This came from Southleigh.

Some years ago a silver cross, now in the church, was found in a garden near the Wesleyan Chapel. This possibly was buried in 1547, so as to keep it out of the clutches of Sir Thomas Bridges, and lost and forgotten. Perhaps the person failed to find the spot where it lay — not like one Harris, who buried the wedges he was using on a tree moot (root or stump). He put up over the place a chip with 'Buried here' written upon it. When he went again he found they were stolen, and on the back of the label was written 'Up and gone'. Hence our local saying, if anything could not be found: 'Like Harris' wedges—up and gone'.

Stanton Harcourt

Ever since Harcourt, the brother of a Saxon king, helped Rollo to invade France the family has persisted all down the years, whilst names of many noble families have disappeared 'like the baseless fabric of a dream'.

One of his descendants married Isabel de Camvile, and with her he had the manor of Stanton, which henceforth became Stanton Harcourt.

The stones standing in the fields from before the dawn of history doubtless gave the name 'Stan Town'. To see them means a good walk from the village to the farthest, but the sight will repay the journey, and the old questions 'Who? How? When?' will be in the mind. But these questions are not to be answered yet.

The remains of the great house, with Pope's Tower, the curious kitchen with no chimney yet all the roof a chimney, the lake, with its tale of a ghost, and the church are all of interest. As we walk up to enter we feel like walking quietly and thoughtfully, as one always should to any house of God, with the thought of the generations of so many famous men who have worshipped there. Much has been recorded, and we will note a few items of what strikes us of this dignified and spacious building which, if it could speak, could tell of knights and nobles, fair ladies — some gay, some pensive and sad.

We enter. North and south doorways are used. In former days one was reserved for men, and one for women. Passing up the lofty nave, we come to what is considered to be the oldest rood screen in England. The ironwork and other detail are worth noting. My old and esteemed friend, John Dawson, told me that when he was an apprentice they had to clean the paint off the screen. 'And,' said he, 'we knocked out the mullions and popped them into the lathe and turned it off.'

Passing through the door a brass (1516) in the floor to the left hand takes our attention. It is remarkable because it looks as though at the end of Ellen Camby's magnificent girdle is pictured a pomadum. If it is, we see she was in the fashion of the day, as it was usual to carry one of these pierced metal boxes, which held a ball of sweet-smelling herbs.

We look through the locked iron gates into the Harcourt Chapel and note that the Wars of the Roses are remembered, one big red rose being on the end of an altar tomb. Why should God's beautiful flowers be mixed up with awful war? High up on the wall is a standard said to have been carried by a Harcourt into and out of Bosworth Field. It used to hang unfurled, but some persons (Americans, did I hear?) found they could reach through the gate and cut pieces off it, so now it is round the pole, safely beyond the reach of profane relic hunters. The Early English windows at the East end, the transepts, the font, the many monuments, all have a story and a message for us.

Here in this church ministered long ago John Gambold, one of John Wesley's early college friends. It is thought Wesley was his curate here for a time. If anyone knows of any entry or signature anywhere that would prove this I should be very much obliged to hear of it. Wesley preached at Stanton Harcourt Church on June 11th, 1738, and his journal records also, February 17th, 1741:

> I left London, I reached Oxford, and leaving my horse there set out on foot for Stanton Harcourt. The night overtook me in about an hour, accompanied with heavy rain. Being wet and weary and not knowing well my way I could not help saying in my heart (though ashamed of my want of resignation to God's will) O that Thou would'st stay the bottles of heaven or at least give me light, or an honest guide or some help in the manner Thou knowest! Presently the rain ceased, the moon broke out, and a friendly man overtook me, who set me upon his own horse, and walked by my side till we came to Mr. Gambold's door.

I wonder who this kind traveller was? And did he know who he was helping?

Wesley walked to Burford the next day, so his stay at his friend Gambold's house was very brief. They had been members together of the 'Holy Club' at Oxford, and whilst Wesley was away in Georgia Gambold wrote of him: 'Mr. John Wesley was always chief manager, for which he was very fit, for not only had he more learning and experience than the rest, but he was blest with such activity as to be always gaining ground and had such steadiness that he lost none.'

Wesley's sister Keziah made her home with Mr Gambold and his sister, for some time before her death, after she had been treated in such shocking fashion by Westley Hall, who proposed to her and then married her sister Martha. The story of that wretched man and his abominable treatment of these two Wesley women is painful and sordid in the extreme. 'Hall was a hawk amongst the doves of the Wesley family,' it has been said.

John Wesley wrote him a long and faithful letter pointing out the steps of his fall:

> You left off going to church as well as to the sacrament ... you began to teach uncommon opinions: as that, there is no resurrection of the body; that there is no general judgment to come, and, that there is no hell, no worm that never dieth, no fire that never shall be quenched. You can eat and drink and be merry ... You are in the very belly of hell: only the pit hath not shut her mouth upon you. Arise, thou sleeper and call upon thy God.

This plain, faithful letter did not turn the fallen clergyman from the downward path. He hurried on, and for many years was an adventurous profligate, acting sometimes as a doctor, sometimes as priest — any character as convenient. When he returned from abroad, after a life of wicked folly, his angel of a wife received him, and in her care he died

Gambold resolved to leave the Church of England and enter the Moravian Church. Lord Harcourt tried to prevail on him to remain, but he printed an address to his parishioners in 1742, and became a bishop in the fellowship of his choice till, twenty-seven years later, after being heard to pray, 'Dear Saviour, remember my poor name and come, come soon,' he went to the Better Land.

POPE

Alexander Pope's associations with Stanton Harcourt are well known. The grey old tower yet bears his name, 'Pope's Tower', but his 'Memoir of P.P., Clerk of this Parish' is not generally known perhaps. Here are a few extracts:

In the name of the Lord, Amen. I, P.P. by the grace of God Clerk of this Parish, writeth this history.

Thou mayest conceive, O reader, with what concern I perceived the eyes of the congregation fixed upon me, when I first took my place at the feet of the Priest. When I raised the Psalm, how did my voice quiver with fear! And when I arrayed the shoulders of the minister with the surplice, how my joints tremble under me... Notwithstanding, it was my good hap to acquit myself to the good liking of the whole congregation, but the Lord forbid I should glory therein.

He tried to improve matters in the church as follows—

I was specially severe in whipping forth dogs from the Temple, all except the lap dog of the good widow Howard, a sober dog which yelped not, nor was there offence in his mouth.

I did even proceed to moroseness, though sore against my heart, unto poor babes, in tearing from them the half-eaten apple, which they privily munched at church. But verily it pitied me, for I remembered the days of my youth.

With the sweat of my own hands I did make plain and smooth the dogs' ears throughout our Great Bible.

I swept the pews, not before swept in the third year. I darned the surplice and laid it in lavender.

Now was the long expected time arrived when the Psalms of King David should be hymned unto the same tunes to which he played them upon his harp, etc., etc.

Did Pope pen this at Stanton Harcourt, and was it a picture more or less of the clerk there?

The tablet on the outer wall of the church recording the two lovers being killed by lightning, is well known.

Our late King, Edward VII, had a look at Stanton Harcourt on Sunday afternoon, June 30th, 1907.

The stocks, with iron straps to hold culprits for whipping or branding with a hot iron, yet stand in the street. They should be protected from the weather to preserve them.

SUTTON

Before the Wesleyan Chapel was built, as many as seventy people have been present at services held in a cottage at Sutton.

Stonesfield

Doomsday records, Stuntesfeld, 1 hide. Aluric (R. de Stratford). Wednesbury is said to have been given to the ancestors of Will de Heronvill in exchange for Stonesfield.

PHELELEIA
FAWLER MONASTERY AND CHURCH OF ST. JOHN.

Charters yet exist with signatures of Richard de Camville and others which show that this Forest Benedictine priory was assigned by Henry I to Eynsham. Stephen renewed the grant, as did the Count of Meulan, who later transferred the monks to Eynsham, the church becoming deserted, and referred to in 1315 as 'la forsaken ho', whilst from the rent returns of John Baldock, the assart of Stonesfield is recorded 1394, and again Charlbury rent collector, William Baugh, records Stonesfield assart 1409. This rent was paid by the men af Stonesfield for the site of the monastery.

In 1528 the Abbey received 25/- from 'assarts in the fields of Fawler leased by the tenants of Stonesfield'.

THE ROMAN VILLA

About 1711, as George Hannes was ploughing in 'Chest Hill Acre', near to Akeman Street, his plough disturbed some stones, and amongst them he found an urn. This he ran home with, leaving his man and horses in the field. Some thought he found money in the urn, but this he denied. On further search he found at about two feet below the surface a tesselated Roman pavement 35 feet by 20 feet, composed of small cubes with six different colours, in patterns, figures and borders.

Again in 1779 the area of several other rooms with pavements as previously found were uncovered, as well as a bath with a pipe of lead. Many roofing slates and mortar and nails were amongst the rubbish that covered the floors.

Drawings were made, and these are in the care of the Society of Antiquaries.

The remains, as far as examined, were of the extent of about 190 feet by 152 feet. If one walks over the site to-day one will notice in the soil pieces of Roman brick or tile.

STONESFIELD CHURCH

The Church of St. James consists of nave, chancel, side aisles and a northern chantry, with a noticeable window in the north wall, with a detached central column, not at all usual in our district.

The shafts in the jambs of the chancel arch and the clustered pillars of the Early English style deserve notice. There are decorated windows. A perpendicular window has been inserted in the western wall of the tower, very wide for its position and was, I should say, a risky thing for the tower, to pierce such a wide opening when the window was inserted. The pulpit was erected in 1629. The old wrought iron clock has recently been replaced by a new one. The old one might have been preserved as a specimen of ancient local craft in the church, or at the museum at Oxford.

STONESFIELD BLIND HOUSE

On the right-hand side of the churchyard entrance gate is the quaint old blind house or lock-up. Most places could only boast of stocks, staff and handcuffs for the rowdy and unruly, but Stonesfield had the distinction of a little prison strongly built of stone, domed over and slated. The door can be seen today, studded with nails, with a grating and a strong hasp for the lock. It has now for long been used as a coal store for the parish church. The stocks used to stand in the street not far away.

THE WINDMILL

Part of this structure is yet standing, though it has not been used as a mill for many years.

METHODISM

Methodism has for many years been a factor in the life of the place. Introduced about 1823, services were held in a cottage, then, I believe, in a barn. In 1827 a site for a chapel was bought for £7 10s. from John Austin. The Revs. John Henley and Corbett Cook were the ministers in charge of the circuit.

William Allen and George Crocker, local preachers, signed the deed. Quite possibly they were the first preachers. There were fifteen members. George

Laughton, a class leader, a beautiful character, a lover of books, figures in early days.

Philip Austin, a local preacher, went under the railway bridge near Ashford Mill to fetch out his tools, and the centre upon which the arch had been turned fell upon him and killed him.

David Barrett told me that as a lad he stood at the window of the cottage during the service, and someone inside asked him to move away and 'let the air come in.' He rudely replied, 'Hare; I can't see any hare.' But in his case, as in many others, the scoffer remained to pray. He became a great singer and musician, could play the bass viol and sing any part. Once he said, 'When I get to heaven I will get one side of the Saviour with my bass viol and King David on the other with his harp, and we will make heaven's arches ring.'

One day as he was walking along with some other men the bell began tolling for someone departed, and he said to those with him, 'Soon it will be, "There goes the bell for old David Barrett; his singing days are over." But they will be wrong — my singing days will be just begun.'

In 1859 he went with George Poole one night to the chapel, and together they knelt in prayer and continued turn and turn about till, looking up, they found the candle end burnt out and they were in the dark. Agreeing to come again in a week they did so, and were presently joined by others. There was a great stir and awakening — only the day will declare it.

Caleb Townsend used to walk over to Finstock and preach to us, his face like the face of an angel.

George Williams — how his ringing voice would arrest all within its range as he told, as he loved to do, the glad tidings.

William Roberts: his sun went down whilst it was yet day, and a host 'who walk with Him in white for they are worthy.'

'They in the joyful rest of Paradise who dwell,
The blessed ones, with joy the chorus swell,
Alleluia!'

The Primitives built a chapel, and a cause was maintained for years. For some time now, however, the building has been used by the Salvation Army as their meeting hall.

STONESFIELD SLATES

Mention must be made of these remarkable slates formerly dug at Stonesfield, but I fear this 'most ancient of Oxfordshire industries' is a thing of the past.

I am glad I went down into some of the mines— 'pits' locally. A shaft about 20 feet deep, like a draw well, with a ladder lashed vertical, and then with bent back crouching along a passage, or gallery, to the workings, all carried on under the most primitive conditions.

The 'slats' were hammered into shape in a little 'Slat house' built from waste with a 'hommer' and a 'peck'. They have been used in all the district, making the beautifully wrinkled roofs that, when coated with the lichens that covered them, for appearance and comfort could not be beaten. On good timbers well 'pointed to the pin,' as filling with lime mortar every crevice on the underside between the rafters was called, they were sound for fifty years or more.

In the winter many men were formerly employed digging, and from Finstock I have been told when the 'Slat diggers' went in the morning they would call to each other 'Rope,' which was the old pit call it seems.

Slates could not be made without the stone got frozen, and as 'Jack Frost' is so uncertain a chap as to when he will work at all, it was quite a chance business, and risks had to be taken. Great rejoicings and much thankfulness was felt after a week's good frost came, and bright looks and warm hearts were at Stonesfield. The fife band paraded once, it is said, in celebration of a good frost.

From the 10th century, it is said, the slates are on record. Those interested in fossils should visit the University Museum at Oxford, and a visit to the vast heaps of slate waste at Stonesfield will well repay them.

OVERSEAS

Stonesfield is represented in many places overseas, and the old place and neighbourhood is not forgotten.

An early settler in Western Australia was Mr. Walter Padbury, a member of a family known for long in our Manor and district. He became a sheep farmer, and was most successful, building a ship to convey his wool to the home land. The ship was called 'The Charlotte Padbury', his wife's name, and it plied to and from this country with his cargoes of wool and goods. At Koojan, where he lived, he built a Church dedicated to St. James, after the church in his native village. When he died he left large bequests to the Cathedral Church at Perth, Western Australia.

ANOTHER STONESFIELD NAME

Austin is a name at Stonesfield that for many years was connected with stone working. The west window in Witney Church, mullions and tracery, and the whole of the stone work was cut by one of the family; and many of the old grave yard memorials in the district were done by men of the same name. When in 1877 a steeple jack from Blackburn climbed the monument in Blenheim Park, he found a big copper penny on the platform upon which the figure of the duke is placed; then climbing up on to the duke's shoulders he sang 'Rule Britannia'. On the arm of the figure he found the name 'J. Austin'.

A Sun Dial

There can be seen on the wall of the house that used to be the Post Office, opposite the Wesleyan Chapel, the place over the door where used to be fixed an interesting sun dial. The words on it as a motto were 'Let not the sun go down upon your wrath'.

Stonesfield Again

In the seventies the Ordnance Survey men used Stonesfield Church tower as an observation post, and had a white tent on top of it that could be seen all round the countryside. I heard at the time a little jingle, something as follows:

'Stonesfield tower wears a hat,
Charlbury tower's no better than that
Field-Town steeple's ready to fall,
But Ramsden steeple beats 'em all.'

Ramsden steeple, 99ft. 2ins. in height, had just been built, and looked like a delicate white finger pointing heavenwards, and Field Town (Leafield) did, I know, have things said about its appearance. It had rather a bulging look. A blacksmith said to me, 'It looks as though it had been clapped on hot.'

Floods

In 1799 a letter written from Fawler Mill (quite near to Stonesfield) says:— 'The water was within two inches of the top step of our front door, and at the back door six inches deep. We had the back door stanked up else we should not have had a dry place to set our feet upon. The water was very deep in our Mill, and we had about 100 sacks wetted. There was never a flood in the memory of man that came into our house before.'

NOTE — Do not destroy old letters, maps, or papers, re our Wychwood district. In your ear — *May I see them?*

Swinbrook

SWINBROC, 1203. SWENEBROCK, 1311.

This pretty little village till quite recently was on the brook, right enough, for all vehicular traffic had to go for many yards down the river bed, the water completely covering the road. A raised causeway for foot passengers was at one side, but all other traffic had to take to the water. A ford leading round to the ancient School is still there, I believe, though the stream as above has during recent years been diverted from the road.

The name is evidently associated with swine, and as mentioned elsewhere they abounded in Wychwood.

The Church is perched on a rising part of the village. The site is well above the stream, as though the early builders thought, at some places nearby in this

The smithy, Swinbrook, with chestnut tree

old forest, others have built God's house too near the water courses. Here is an ideal spot. It is dedicated to St. Mary. It consists of nave, aisles, and chancel with western tower. The magnificent Fettiplace monuments, figures tier on tier, brasses, etc., are together with the fine oak stalls with quaint misereres (turn the seats up and see), one of the sights of our forest border churches.

The great Fettiplace family (one of them was Mayor of Oxford on ten occasions) owned Manors in fifteen counties. The well-known lines give this:

'The Traceys, the Lacys, and the Fettiplaces

Own all the woods, the parks and the chases.'

The family is now extinct, and even the Mansion has gone. It was the home of a party of robbers and highwaymen, if report be true, after the noble family had quitted it.

There are considerable charities at this place.

I have a nice little early bronze flat-shaped taper holder, or candlestick, found amongst some ashes underneath a hearth stone in a house near the church. How did it get there? An easier one please!

The Primitive Methodists have a chapel here, and very worthy men have got inspiration and strength to walk life's pathway in association with the worship there.

Just to the west of the Church, near the field path leading to Widford, are terraces plainly to be seen in the fields where possibly were the grounds of the ancient Mansion.

Widford Church of St. Oswald was in a sorry state (it was unused) when I first visited it, but in 1904 it was made weather proof. It is on the site of a Roman Villa, to judge by the remains that have been found when digging in the churchyard.

A Violin Maker

A shoe maker used to make fiddles here. He carved a human face on his fiddle necks, where the scrolls usually are.

The Village Dentist

At the quaint blacksmith's shop for some fifty years Mr. House, the smith, extracted teeth. He sold me his homemade key after he had got past using it. He sold me, too, a very large door lock with a key a foot in length.

Taynton and Tangly

Formerly of great repute for its free stone used for grand masonry at all the important buildings in the neighbourhood; many tombs, those with the big tops favoured by the Cotswold wool men, being fashioned from it.

There are many houses worth looking at in the place. The mason family of Strongs, who were of such account as mentioned elsewhere, were born and had their early training here, at Taynton, as stone cutters.

The Church of St. John has various features. Early English, Decorated and Perpendicular work is to be seen, as well as Rood stairs, a squint and monuments.

Not far away is Tangly, a big massive house, looking as though it could stand a siege, and its lonely position in wild, lawless days, needed a place that would be strong and safe. The big door has a crudely cut hole in it, covered on the inside with an iron plate. The story is that robbers one night cut this hole, and one inserted his arm to unfasten the door. Someone inside grasped it, and with a cord made it fast. Despite the frantic efforts of the, robbers the hand was held secure, and there was nothing for it but to cut it off, which was done, leaving the hand within the door so that the robber could get away.

At Tangly oxen were ploughing in the field when I was there some years ago. They used to be used for that purpose at Finstock. Joseph Guy and others used to ride on their backs to and from the field. Now ugly tractors bang and pant, both sight and sound an abomination amongst our peaceful surroundings.

Wilcote

In a charter to Cogges Priory, 1103, it is spelt Wilecote.

William Willicotes had custody of Wychwood forest for Henry IV. He founded an obit (anniversary) at Spelsbury Church, where he was buried in 1410. His seal was at the Bodleian, inscribed

Sigillu Thome de Wylkote Armigeri

with arms as on the Wilcote Chapel at Northleigh Church.

In 1448-9 Henry VI made Ralph Boteler master forester for life, vert and venison all to be his. The Boteler family lived at Wilcote, their mansion being called Boteler's Court.

Coins and abundance of fragments of pottery found at Wilcote show that it was favoured by early settlers.

THE CHURCH

This Church of St. Peter is worth seeing. It is entered by a north porch, and consists of nave and chancel. A blocked-up arch shows there was formerly a transept chapel. A very good Norman doorway, walled up, is on the south side. An Early English window and decorated windows, with a bell-cote aloft on the western gable, all give interest to this tiny church set amidst green fields, trees and wild flowers, 'far from the madding crowd.'

LORD WILCOTE'S GHOST

The field below Wilcote House (where is a cottage) used to be called 'Nor-lye lotments,' and the story is that Lord Wilcote (whose effigy is carved in Northleigh Church) left it as a charity to the poor, and they were unjustly defrauded of it. Lord Wilcote could not rest, and it was said he was seen riding in his carriage through the air at night, fire snorting out of the nostrils of the horses. As he rode along he held up his finger, saying 'Cast up; cast up.' One night he came near enough to the earth for the foot of one of the horses to touch a big stone over a stream in front of Bridewell Farm House. It was said that the print of a hoof was left in the stone. I went as a boy with my father one day to see this mark, but to my great regret the stone had been taken away.

A number of clergymen met at Wilcote to learn from his lordship what should be done in order that his spirit should remain at rest. One naturally thinks the reply would be 'Restore the charity,' but instead he is reported to have said, 'Destroy the bell in Wilcote Church and I shall not come again.' The bell was forthwith removed and sent to be re-cast, whilst the clapper was thrown into Wilcote Pool. When the pool was cleaned out the clapper was found, but it was thrown in again. Such is the story I heard from my dear old grandmother, whose mother, Mrs. Day, was formerly housekeeper at Wilcote.

People used to walk across the fields from Finstock to the church, it being nearer than Charlbury. When I was a lad I used to trudge the same pleasant paths carrying a large square basket, lined with snow-white cloths, to fetch butter, laid in green dock leaves. This journey was undertaken for Mrs. Eeles, at the shop, and for it I had twopence per week.

In one of the rooms at the farm was stored a Sedan chair, and never shall I forget seeing some pictures in a copy of Foxe's *Martyrs*. In the kitchen a number of flitches of bacon used to be hung end up from one part of the ceiling. It was lofty, and there was room to walk underneath. I often used to wonder what damage would be done should one of the cords happen to break. There was a mess room with plain stools for the farm men to sit for their meals, and a big boiler of hot milk for them to drink.

When the late Mr. C. Sartoris, of Wilcote House, filled in the gaps between Topples and the other woods at Wilcote by planting trees, in the seventies, he said he would like to come back in a hundred years time and see the effect of his work. A sight of the splendid stretch of massed tree beauty from the Fawler and the Stonesfield roads is quite enough to justify his desire. It is glorious.

Witney

WITNIE, Doomsday; WITNEYE, 1045.

In 1268 Eynsham Abbey contracts to sell the Abbey wool to Roger Harang, of Wytten, and in a claim about their assart and woods mention is made of Wyttene in connection with Wichwode, May 20th, 1325.

'Wytney, part of Wichwode Forest,' so writes an old author long ago, and no doubt the forest traditions, habits and laws played a big part in the life of the town in days of yore. The love of venison always persisted at Witney, and the money in circulation there, when most forest border villages near were hard pushed to live, made it a welcome market. If daring men would convey the deer when killed, purchasers were waiting to buy, and in the night many a lot of venison was carried to this thriving place. Witney, like Isaac, said 'Give me meat such as my soul loveth,' and they had it.

An old proverb says 'Witney, famous for four B's — beauty, bread, beer and blankets.'

WITNEY CHURCH

Witney Church is a building which gives pleasure to the beholder, whether seen from the town or (perhaps best of all) from the station way. This fine church will repay time and thought given to its study, whether viewed as a whole or in detail. Norman, Early English, Perpendicular and Decorated styles greet you and ask for inspection. Foreign influence is considered to be evident in the design of the beautiful spire with its entrancing lines; also the flamboyant tracery in the window, as you approach the entrance from the town, is noticeable at once.

The positions of many altars formerly in use within make us think of the dim ages when men thought of the simple memorial sacrament as a sacrifice, and priest and mass were to the fore.

Taken as a whole, one admires greatly the spacious, dignified, beautiful building, the work of builders who have gone, and we think of Him

'Whose Temple is the arch of yon unmeasured sky,

Whose Sabbath, the tremendous march of vast eternity.'

February 3rd, 1643, was celebrated at Oxford by the ringing of bells and rejoicings, for Prince Rupert had taken Cirencester, capturing about seven hundred prisoners. These were imprisoned in the church there for two days, food being handed to them by friends through the windows. They were tied together and marched through slush and snow, and on reaching Witney they were imprisoned in the church, and no doubt made themselves as comfortable as such quarters allowed. They were not allowed to leave the building during the time the Royalist soldiers kept them there. So Witney Church saw life in its stern, difficult and painful side in those terrible days.

WITNEY, WRITTEN ABOUT 1771

In the hundred of Bampton is a long straggling, uncouth, but populous and large town, with a market on Thursday, and six annual fairs, viz., Easter-Thursday, Holy Thursday, July 10th, Thursday before October 10th, Thursday after the 8th September, and December 4th, for horses, cows, pigs, and various commodities.

It is a borough town, governed by two bailiffs chosen annually on the first Tuesday after St. Michael. This town was of good repute before the conquest and, in the fifth and eighth of Edward II sent members to Parliament, which it continued till the thirty-third of Edward III and no longer.

The Post Office is kept by Mr. Richard Ashfield, into which all letters must be put by seven o'clock in the evening or subject to payment of a penny each; the postage on letters from London to this place is sixpence, and are delivered out at about eight o'clock in the morning.

The town is situated in the turnpike road leading from London to Gloucester, Bath, Bristol, and Cheltenham; distance from London sixty-four miles, Gloucester thirty-six miles, Bath fifty-six miles, Bristol fifty-nine miles, Cheltenham twenty-seven miles.

Here are at work one hundred and fifty looms continually for which above three thousand people from eight years old and upwards are daily employed in carding, spinning, &c., and consume about eighty packs of wool weekly. The blankets are usually ten or twelve quarters wide, and very white, which some attribute to the abstertive nitrous waters of the river Windrush wherewith they are scoured; but others believe it is owing to a peculiar way of loose spinning they use here, and others again are of opinion that it proceeds from both. In consequence of which this town has engrossed the whole trade in that commodity.

They likewise make here the Duffield stuffs a yard and three-quarters wide, which are carried to New England and Virginia, and much worn over there in winter. Here is likewise a great many fellmongers, who, having dressed and stained their sheep-skins, make them into jackets and breeches, and sell them at Bampton; from whence they are dispersed all over the neighbouring counties.

The company of blanket-weavers in Witney and its vicinity are by letters patent, granted in the tenth year of the reign of Queen Anne, incorporated by the name of 'The master, assistants, wardens, and commonalty, of blanket weavers inhabiting in Witney in the County of Oxford, or within 20 miles thereof'; by virtue of which they enjoy the sole right of manufacturing blankets of every kind in the town of Witney, or within 20 miles of the same. This company consists of a master and two wardens, who are elected annually, and about 20 assistants, and 50 of the commonalty. They have a common hall in Witney, where they transact all matters and things relative to the rules and orders of the company, and several men are there employed to examine, weigh, measure, and mark, all goods that are made by the company, and, if any be found deficient in weight or measure, a very heavy fine is imposed on, and paid by the makers thereof: which regular and uniform mode of examining the goods, and the forcing the making of them, the full weight and measure together with their peculiar method of manufacturing them, have always rendered the goods of this manufactory superior in quality to any of the kind in the world.

This neighbourhood produces a sort of yellow ochre, and a coarse kind of gritty umber which is of great use to leather dressers.

The river Windrush runs through the town, over which there is an ancient stone bridge erected.

The church, pleasantly situated at the south end of the town, is a large and noble edifice in the Gothic taste. The steeple is very justly admired for its exact symmetry and proportion, and allowed by all travellers who see it to be a curious specimen of just and correct architecture.

The tower contains a peal of eight bells.

The rectory is worth £800 a year.

Witney was one of the manors which Alwinus, bishop of Winchester, gave to the Church of St. Swithin there, on Queen Emma's passing over the fire ordeal.

A bank is established here, under the firm of Messrs. Leake, Bath, Sanders and Holton.

Here is a large free school and fine library; Rev. Mr. Seele, head master, salary £30 per annum; the Rev. Mr. Powell, usher, salary £15 per annum. A writing master attends one hour in the day, salary £10 per annum, besides perquisites.

Here is an hospital also for six poor blanket-makers' widows, and a school for twelve poor children, founded in 1723, to which has been made an addition for teaching thirty children.

Here is one very capital inn for the accommodation of the nobility, gentry, &c. Here are likewise several other good inns for the accommodation of travellers, besides a great number of public-houses.

Two coaches pass through Witney every day: one of them leaves the Angel Inn, behind St. Clement's Church, and the other the Bolt and Tun, Fleet Street, every day at noon, and pass through Witney about one o'clock the next morning in their way to Gloucester, &c., and return every day, through Witney in their way to London, the one about nine, the other about eleven o'clock in the evening. There are constantly two or more waggons leave Witney every Monday afternoon, which get into London on Wednesday, leave London on Thursday, and return to Witney on Saturday about noon. The following are the principal inhabitants:

GENTRY, &c.

Beechy, Walter, *Gent.*

Collins, John,   "

Druce, Samuel,   "

Lankshear, Thos., *Gent.*

Maddock, Robt.,   "

Symmonds, Thos.,   "

Witts, Parish Rich., *Gent.*

CLERGY

Collins, Rev. Wm.

Phipps, Rev. Weston, Rector.

Seele, Rev. Mr., *Master of the Free School.*

PHYSIC

Batt, Ed., *Surgeon,* &c.

Lanksheer, Wm., *Surgeon,* &c.

Trimnel, John, *Surgeon,* &c.

LAW

Leake, John, *Attorney.*

Ward, Chas., *Attorney.*

Macey, Wm., *Attorney and Coroner.*

TRADERS

Andrews, Mrs., *Innholder.*

Ashfield, Rich., *Postmaster.*

Bolton, Hy., *Blanket Weaver.*

Baker, John, *Locksmith.*

Banting, Wm., *Baker.*

Breakspear, Mrs., *Slater.*

Barnes, Wm., *Blacksmith.*

Barrett, Wm., *Shoemaker.*

Biggers, Jeremiah, *Blanket Weaver.*

Birdseye, Wm. *Blacksmith.*

Bolton, Ed., *Common Brewer.*

Bolton, Henry, *Victualler.*

Bolton, Thos., *Victualler.*

Brigstock, Joseph., *Farmer.*

Brooks, John., *Blanket Weaver.*

Broome, Wm., *Mercer.*

Brown, John, *Butcher.*

Brown, W., *Plumber & Glazier.*

Castle, Jas., *Slater.*

Charlwood, Sarah, *Baker & Maltster*

Clark, John, *Taylor.*

Clark, Thos.   "

Clark, Wm., *Cooper.*

Clinch, John, *Staymaker.*

Coburn, Isaac, *Innholder.*

Collins, Jn., *Blanket Weaver.*

Collins, Thos.,   "   "

Collier, Ed., *Taylor.*

Collier, Ed., *Butcher.*

Collier, Jn., Blanket Weaver.

Collier, Rich.,   "   "

Collier, Robt.,   "   "

Collier, Wm.,   "   "

Cook, Wm.   "   "

Cowell, Josiah, *Breeches Maker.*

Coxeter, Thos., *Blanket Weaver.*

Cripps, Michael, *Hemp Dresser.*

Daily, Thos. & Wm., *Farmers &
Carriers*

Dix, John, *Blanket Weaver.*

Dix., Thos., *Carpenter.*

Druce, Ed., *Grocer & Tallow
Chandler.*

Druce, Thos., *Blanket weaver.*

Dutton, John, *Blanket weaver.*

Dutton, Joseph, *Shoemaker.*

Dyer, Rich., *Blanket Weaver.*

Early, Ed.,   "   "

Early, Jn., sen.,   "   "

Early, Jn., jun.,   "   "

Eeles, Wm.,   "   "

Ellis, John, *Taylor.*

Ellis, Wm., *Mercer & Draper.*

Empson, Thos., *Blanket Weaver.*

Farden, John, *Mercer & Maltster.*

Fisher, Bartholomew, *Wool Factor.*

Fisher, Bartholonew, *Felmonger.*

Fisher, Chas., *Cooper.*

Fisher, John, *Blanket Weaver.*

Fisher, Rich., *Maltster.*

Fisher, Robt., *Blanket Weaver.*

Fitchett, John, *Peruke-maker.*

Gadfield, Henry, *Breeches Maker.*

Green, Wm., *Milkman.*

Hambridge, Geo., sen., *Butcher.*

Hambridge, Geo., jun.   "

Hampshear, Wm., *Brazier.*

Hankins, E., *Blanket Weaver.*

Hankins, Jas., *Pawnbroker.*

Hankins, John, *Blanket Weaver.*

Hanks, John, *Narrow Weaver.*

Hartshorn, Dan., *Blanket Weaver.*

Harris, Thos., *Carpenter & Joiner.*

Hathaway, George, *Blanket Weaver.*

Haynes, John, *Baker.*

Haynes, Robert, *Shoemaker.*

Hewer, John, *Blanket Weaver.*

Hewer, Samuel, *Felmonger.*

Higgins, Samuel, *Oxford Carrier.*

Hiscock, R., *Blanket Weaver &
Ironmonger.*

Hobbs, Jas., *Taylor and Breeches
Maker.*

Holton, Jas., *Mealman.*

Hudson, John, *Baker.*

Jackson, Wm., *Blacksmith.*

Jeffry, John, *Blanket Weaver.*

Kearse, John, *Felmonger.*

Kearse, Wm., *Breeches Maker.*

Lucket, Thos., *Plumber & Glasier.*

Lardner, Rich., *Blanket Weaver.*

Long, Wm., *Carpenter, &c.,*

Marriott, Wm., *Blanket Weaver.*

Marriott, Wm., *Maltster.*

Matthews, *Blanket Weaver.*

Mazey, Chas., *Watch & Clock Maker.*

May, John, *Watch & Clock Maker.*

Miles, Walter, *Carrier.*

Moreton, Sammons, *Blanket Weaver.*

Morris, Robt., *Grocer.*

Morris, Thos., *Blanket Maker.*
Pain, Rich., *Timber Merchant.*
Parme, John, *Blanket Weaver.*
Partlet, Job, *Blanket Weaver.*
Prior, Wm., *Shoemaker.*
Pruce, Jonathan, *Felmonger.*
Reade, Ed., *Excise Officer.*
Richard, Cobwin, *Clothier.*
Read[i]ng, Rich., *Woolstapler.*
Rose, Ed., *Grocer.*
Rowles, John, *Mason.*
Sanders, Chas., *Common Brewer.*
Seeley & Shorter, *Blanket Weavers.*
Sheppard, Wm., *Blanket Weaver.*
Shorter, John, *Blanket Weaver.*
Shorter, Wm., *Baker & Dyer.*
Shuffrey, John, sen., *Blanket Weaver.*
Shuffrey, John, jun., *Blanket Weaver.*
Smith, John, *Felmonger.*
Smith, Rich., *Baker.*
Smith, Thos., *Innholder.*
Smith, Thos., *Hatter.*
Smith, Thos., *Blanket Weaver.*
Smith, Wm., *Innholder & Joiner.*
Spittle,Wm., *Baker.*
Stevens, John, *Butcher.*
Swingburn, Thos., *Mealman.*
Symonds, Mrs., *Grocer & Mercer.*

Tanner, Wm., *Gardener.*
Taylor, Thos., *Maltster.*
Tempany, John, *Peruke-maker.*
Thurley, Thos., *Carpenter.*
Trundell, Benj., *Victualler.*
Turner, Wm., *Bookseller.*
Waine, Henry, *Shoemaker.*
Waine, Thos., *Blanket Weaver.*
Waine, Wm., sen., *Blanket Weaver.*
Waine, Wm., jun., *Blanket Weaver.*
Wainwright, Geo., *Butcher.*
Webb, Mary, *Mercer.*
Wells, John, *Sheriff's Officer.*
Wells, John, *Currier.*
Wells, Richard, *Grocer.*
Whitlocke, *Blanket Weaver.*
Whiting,Wm.   ”   ”
Wilkinson, G., *Carpenter, Weaver, Joiner, &c.*
Williams, Geo., *Narrow Weaver.*
Williams, Thos., *Baker.*
Wiggins, Thos., *Wheeler.*
Wright, Samuel, *Victualler.*
Wright, Samuel, *Cornfactor.*
Woodington, John, *Baker.*
Woods, William, *Mercer, Draper & Auctioneer.*

LAW AND ORDER

Punishment for breaking the law was often carried out on the spot, and transgressors caught red-handed were dealt with whilst the blood was up.

Galley (Gallows) Hill, where is now the cemetery, not so long ago had its gibbets standing.

The constable, at about 20/- per year, saw to the peace of the place, with staff, handcuffs, stocks, and his terrible whip for bare-back treatment. He got one shilling for stopping a fight, but the rule was 'Do not hurry on the scene; let them fight it out themselves a bit.' Prize fighting was left to the lowest and most abandoned. A noted prize fighter, it is said, fought some local champion at White Oak Green, but these things were most rightly thought a shame, as the following will show:

The parish clerk at one of our villages died suddenly on his way home from seeing a prize fight. The clergyman would not have the bells used at the funeral, to show his displeasure, but on Sunday it was found that most of the clappers had been removed from the bells, and they were fished up some weeks later from a deep hole in the bed of the river Evenlode.

A Witney Quakers' Marriage Certificate

Whereas William Maddock, shoemaker, of Witney, in the County of Oxon, son of Edmund Maddock, maltster, deceased, of Fulbrook in the county aforesaid, And Sarah Pottinger, spinster, daughter of Rich. Pottinger, husbandman, deceased of Adderbury in the County aforesaid, Having Publickly declared their Intentions of taking each other in Marriage before several meetings of the People called Quakers in Witney aforesaid according to the good order used among them, whose Proceedings therein, after a deliberate Consideration thereof (with Regard unto the Righteous Law of God, and Example of his People Recorded in the Scriptures of truth in that Case) were approved by the said Meetings, they appearing clear of all others, and having also Consent of Relatives and Parties concerned. Now these are to certifie all whom it may concern, That for the Accomplishing of their Intentions this eighteenth day of the fifth Month called July in the year One Thousand Seven Hundred and Fifty They the said William Maddock and Sarah Pottinger appeared in a public assembly of the aforesaid People and others, met together for that purpose in their Public Meeting Place at Chipping Norton in ye County aforesaid and in a solemn Manner He the said Wm. Maddock taking the said Sarah Pottinger by the Hand did openly declare as followeth, *'Friends in the fear of God and in the presence of this Assembly I take this my friend Sarah Pottinger to be my Wife promising thro Divine Assistance to be unto her a loving faithfull Husband till Death separate us.'* And then and there in the said assembly the said Sarah Pottinger did in like manner declare as followeth, *'Friends, in the fear of God and in the presence of this Assembly, I take this my friend William Maddock to be my husband promising thro Divine assistance to be unto him a loving and faithful wife till Death separate us.'* And the said William Maddock and Sarah Pottinger as a further Confirmation thereof, did then, and there, to these Presents set their Hands. And We whose Names are hereunto subscribed, being present amongst others at the Solemnizing of the above mentioned Marriage and Subscription in manner aforesaid as Witnesses thereunto have also to these Presents Subscribed our Names the Day and Year above written.

Thomas Right. Simon Holford. John Hopkins. William Norson. Nicholas
Harris. John Gibbs. Elizabeth Adkins. Hannah Summerfield. Han.
Squire. Ann Clark. Jane Busby. Shusanah Hoyte. William Maddock.
Sarah Pottinger. Robt. Maddock. John Pottinger. Thos. Pottinger. Robt.
Maddock, Jun. Wm. Hill. Mary Freeman.

TOBACCO DESTROYED

An old document gives particulars and expenses of an official, John
Cutteford, sent in Charles II's day to destroy English grown tobacco in this
district, as the Act directs, 1668: —

July 30. It. At Witney wheare Justice Gunn and Justice Hoard issued out
their warrants for Bampton hundred.
Thurs., 31. — I went to Stanlake wheare the quantity of 26 akers was the
last yeare, but this yeare was none but a few plants in one garden wch was
distroyed. £4 14s. 6d. At Witney in all 5 dayes and nights for 4 men and
2 horses £11 0s. 9d.'
August 4. — To Burford wheare I searched Sir John Lentall's house and
Gardens but found no tobacco. Stayed there one night, 4 men and 2 horses.
13s. 9d.

JOHN WESLEY AND WITNEY

Though he must have passed through it many times, Wesley does not appear
to have preached at Witney till 1764, when he was 61 years old and well on with
his evangel.

There was an independent chapel there, and his dictum was 'Go to those that
need you most.'

His journal describes an adventurous crossing of the river flood at Eynsham,
and then his pleasure over his Witney preaching service. A year later he is much
pleased: 'After the service they silently and quietly walked home.'

It was now on his round, and some twenty-four visits are recorded, and he
sent many letters to Nancy Bolton. (The letter given in *Notes on Charlbury* had
been privately printed in the Journal of the Wesley Historical Society.) It
appears Wesley lent to her a grey horse of his, and desired her to ride daily, she
being in poor health. Her friend was a Mrs. Langford. Richard Harbud, Joseph
Purser (class leader) and others lived and died in the faith.

Mr. Valton was an early preacher Wesley appointed. His journal records how
once when preaching a robin redbreast flew and settled twice on his head.

Mrs. Payne, of Fawler Mill, was a daughter of one of the Edens, of
Honeybourne. Wesley records: 'I preached at the side of Mr. Eden's house.' A
little 'Garden of Eden' was thereabout. At Fawler Mill they had prayers and

Bible reading at a quarter to six on summer mornings, in winter at seven o'clock.

Mr. Payne was a musician. My father has told me how the strains from his keyed bugle used to come up to Finstock as he stood playing it at the open mill door. One of his sons, I believe, was at Waterloo. A letter of 1800, to Mrs. Payne, records her brother being present at the opening of Witney Chapel.

FINDING WESLEY ASLEEP

The late Mr. Caleb Harwood told me he heard Mr. Payne tell how he once found Mr. Wesley asleep under the big pear tree (yet standing) in Bolton's orchard, at Finstock.

An old jingle gives another touch:—

'From Finstock Heath to Fawler Mill,
A boy went home to eat and fill;
At supper time he was quite well,
But in the night, O! what befel?'

WESLEY'S LAST LETTER?

The story is that Wesley wrote an open letter to Witney friends, handing it to Mr. Payne and Mr. Bolton to convey (they were at meetings at Banbury). On looking over the letter before starting for home they found they could not read it. It was late, and Wesley had retired. His man, through the bedroom door, told the trouble. Wesley said, 'You read it to them.' 'I cannot, sir,' replied the man. 'Bring it in to me.' On this being done Wesley said, 'I cannot read it myself and I will not write another.'

WITNEY CIRCUIT

Witney was made a circuit in 1803. An old Plan (1826) gives names: COOK, HUNT, R. EARLY, J. EARLY, BUSWELL (of Burford, portrait in vestry there), THOMAS, GARDNER, WILLIS, HARRISON (Charlbury), CROCKETT (Charlbury), JUDD (Freeland, became a minister).

AN UNRECORDED WESLEY PREACHING

The late Mr. John Weller, at 96 years old, told Mr. George Adams, of Bladon, over fifty years ago, that he heard Wesley preach in a barn at Freeland.

THE CIRCUIT HORSE

In the sixties a horse was bought for £14, used for circuit journeys for fourteen years, and then sold for £28.

PRIMITIVE METHODISM

In many of our Wychwood places the Primitive Methodists are in evidence, and there is no doubt this movement has been a power in the religious life of rural England.

The Wesleyan Conference in 1819 declared camp meetings as 'highly improper, and likely to be of considerable mischief.' Hugh Bourne was struck off from membership of the Burslem Quarterly Meeting. He and his friends formed themselves into a society which spread like wildfire, for at the Conference in 1823 there were reported 45 circuits, 202 travelling preachers, 1,435 local preachers, and 29,472 members.

John Wesley after twenty-four years reported 40 circuits, 104 preachers, 25,914 members.

Witney became a circuit town, though it was a question at the time as to whether Charlbury should not have that honour and the minister reside there.

A STAPLE HALL STORY

When, in the old days, this was an inn a couple arrived by the coach and asked if they could stay, and were told they could. The landlady of the house thought as she looked at them, 'I should not wonder if you are a couple just married and on your honeymoon.' It got talked about downstairs and the query was how this question was to be solved. Buttons said he thought he could find out when he took in their tea. This was taken in, and instead of hurrying away Buttons busied himself at the fire or other little things till they had started tea. Presently he arrived, beaming, in the kitchen, bearing the news that it was, as the landlady had surmised, a honeymoon couple. 'How did you find it out ?' she asked. 'Easily enough,' he replied. 'I waited till I heard her say "How many lumps of sugar do you like, my dear?" and I knew unless they were just married she would not have asked that question. She would have known it without asking long ago.'

Woodstock

WUDESTOCK, WUDESTOC. — The place in a wood.

From earliest times this beautiful bit of country throbbed with life and interest. A flint hammer stone, also a fine flint tool and other objects of the Neolithic period which I possess, picked up from the soil, show that early man was here.

'Woodstock, Cornberie, demesne forests of the king.' Doomsday Book.

The greatest in the land have lived, loved, fought or hunted in its borders. Ethelred, 866; Alfred, translating; Edward I, a parliament and the birth of a son; Edward III. and his boys.

The men of the town to carry hay and store for the King's deer, 7d. a day and the cart bed full of hay, at night, as pay.

Hugh de Plesset, not far away, after hanging sundry people on his gallows found himself in prison for stealing does in Wychwood.

Beckett began here what cost him his life.

Geoffry Chaucer, the poet, was a page boy when Queen Phillipa had her court at Woodstock.

Rosamund Clifford, a charming girl of fifteen, caught the fancy of Henry II, and the 'Maze' story came along.

Shakespeare, passing through on his way to and from Oxford, would find something to fill his poet's eye.

Elizabeth, as her sister's prisoner, listened to the song of a Woodstock milk-maid, lowly, poor, but free. Later, in her great days as Queen, she enjoyed the delights of the neighbourhood, visiting her old courtier, Sir Henry Lee, at Lee's Rest and Ditchley.

The Civil War, with guns, marchings and counter marchings; the news that made a thrill: 'April, 1646: Woodstock has fallen.'

Earl Rochester died at High Lodge, repentant, trusting in a crucified Redeemer.

James II resided at the Manor House. Later the house and park (the first in the land to have a wall about it) were given to John, Duke of Marlborough, after the Blenheim victory, 1704. It is now called Blenheim Park, with Palace. The latter is a grand structure built by Vanberg. The Cornbury stone used gives the orange tint. Taynton stone was used for bases and oversailing courses, capped by Portland stone. Let those who pick holes in Vanberg's work build something better.

Some years ago, at a near-by village, a Methodist class leader went to visit a sick member, and found the then Duke of Marlborough there on the same errand. Said his Grace, 'I will read a portion and then (to the class leader) you pray.' He then read the fourteenth chapter of St. John's gospel, and they knelt together in prayer in the cottage bed room.

OLD AND NEW WOODSTOCK
The town to-day is comprised of Old and New Woodstock, separated by the Glyme stream.

TRADERS' TOKENS
In the seventeenth century several traders issued tokens.

A RING
A poesy ring with inscription, 'Remember the covenant,' was found in 1722.

THE BELL FOUNDRY, 1626
Bells at Oxford, Stow-on-Wold and other places bear the names of Richard and Jas. Keen, who did this work here for half a century.

The Glovers

Woodstock gloves, famous for centuries, are still made and sent to all parts.

Woodstock Steel

Watch chains and trinkets, very highly prized, used to be cleverly fashioned here. Though the workers and their craft have gone their work abides, the delight of discerning eyes.

The Beadle's Staff

The above, painted blue, with spike at end, and the Royal and Woodstock arms upon it, is in my possession. Thomas, Duke of Gloucester, had the Woodstock tree stump as his arms, being born there.

The Grammar School

Richard Cornwell, 1585, left money to found a school. Many others have left bequests.

The Church

The church has an interesting west porch and a curious Norman south door. The tower, of classic design, was built in 1784 for £836, by Steve Townsend and J. Churchill. The font spent some of its time in a garden.

Woodstock Church in past days had its sluggard waker and dog whipper who, armed with a long wand, walked about the church in slippers. Those who were nodding felt the stick and had to wake up.

A worthy parish clerk was John Bennett, shoemaker, of Woodstock, who was a poet. His poems, published in 1774, had a great sale. Some of his lines:

'His awl and pen with readiness be found,

To make or keep our understandings sound.'

He was a remarkable, self-taught man. He died in 1803.

The Baptist Chapel

Formerly a day school was attached to this place of worship.

The Methodists

The Wesleyans have a good chapel, with an organ.

At the time of the disruption some of the local friends took sides with the reform party. They were told they must 'Pray, pay and obey.' The latter they did not think it right to do, the Oxford minister put his pen through several names, and so 'Olivet Chapel' and Cause, came into being.

All have done good work. Worthy souls have walked in the high places of thought and life in both bodies — a power for good in the life of the town, there is no doubt.

Wootton

This village, perched upon a hill and spreading over the stream towards the forest of Wychwood, was long ago under its jurisdiction and laws.

In 1382 it formed, with Shipton and other places, part of the marriage dowry of Anne of Bohemia (sister of King Wenceslas IV), who became the wife of Richard II. They were both fifteen years of age. John atte Haithe, of Handborough, helped to manage this property for her. She introduced side saddles for ladies. Richard's badge, the 'White Hart', is still in use as an inn sign in this neighbourhood. Richard was here in 1390. She died in 1394, and Richard mourned her loss with bitter grief.

Akeman Street is near by, and there is a spring which is thought to have medicinal qualities.

The church stands well for appearance, helping to form quite a typical village scene when viewed from the Woodstock to Chipping Norton road. The church reveals Early English, Decorated and Perpendicular features. There is a sundial, 1623, with Latin words upon it.

Bruern Abbey had the advowson by royal gift in 1440.

King Charles I thought to embrace this place within the Forest jurisdiction as in King John's day, but found it could not be done.

Hugh Bourne, the Primitive Methodist leader, once stayed at Wootton, and this body, with the Wesleyan Methodists, have contributed to the religious life of the village.

High Lodge as seen from Finstock Heath across Wychwood Forest.

Conclusion

The sketch of High Lodge, as seen from Finstock Heath, across the Forest, must head our words of conclusion.

Mine has been the joy of the scribe. Places, buildings, books, old letters, Parish papers, parchments, memories, kind friends, have yielded of their store, and with the printer's aid these fragments of Wychwood's story are yours.

In this day of locomotion we must not forget the pure and inexpensive joys that are at our very feet. In many ways 'blessed is he that abideth where he is.'

The woodland scene, the sweep of the countryside, the stars of God o'erhead, the flowers of the field, 'the hawthorn banks of Evenlode,' all can give impressions to the spirit of lowly, unlettered, untravelled souls; such glow of heart words cannot describe, money cannot buy, that some who view them with pity, and perhaps with contempt, may never have known.

If any word of mine shall lead a boy or girl to linger and look, and catch the glint, and go on the wonder quest in our Wychwood country, mine is joy indeed.

FAREWELL, GENTLE READER.

About The Wychwood Press

The Wychwood Press publishes books of local interest, particularly (though not exclusively) of relevance to the area of the Oxfordshire Cotswolds within the medieval royal forest of Wychwood. This is an area loosely bounded by the towns of Witney, Woodstock, Chipping Norton and Burford, and includes the valleys of the Evenlode and Windrush.

Our first books are the present volume, together with *Wychwood: The Evolution of a Wooded Landscape* by Beryl Schumer.

Forthcoming titles will include, we hope, re-issues of John Kibble's other works, including *Charlbury and its Nine Hamlets: Chadlington, Chilson, Coate, Fawler, Finstock, Pudlicote, Shorthampton, Tappewell, and Walcot, with Spelsbury* (to include Jesse Clifford's *My Reminiscences of Charlbury*, written in 1891-1892: Clifford was headmaster of the British School in Charlbury from 1842 to 1884); *The History of Charlbury* by Lois Hey; and an updated and abridged edition of Vernon Watney's rare work, *Cornbury and the Forest of Wychwood*, presently being undertaken by Charles Tyzack. We also plan a book of art and craft as practised in the area today.

We welcome ideas for further titles, and will be glad to hear your suggestions. Please write to Jon Carpenter at The Wychwood Press, 2 The Spendlove Centre, Charlbury OX7 3PQ, or phone or fax 01608 811969. We will be happy to add you to our mailing list for advance information about new titles as they are published.